LAND O LAKES®
COLLECTOR™ SERIES

Pasta!

Pasta With Mixed Salad Greens & Raspberries, page 28

Acknowledgments

LAND O LAKES®
COLLECTOR™ SERIES

Land O'Lakes, Inc.

Lydia Botham, *Test Kitchens/Consumer Affairs Director*
Becky Wahlund, *Managing Food Editor*
Mary Sue Peterson, *Coordinating Food Editor*
Becky Falk, *Marketing Manager*

Russ Moore & Associates, Inc.

Russ Moore, *Publisher*
Richard Cross, *General Manager*
Carla Waldemar, *Executive Editor*
Nancy McDonough, *Art Director*
Kathleen Keuler Bauwens, *Graphic Design Director*
Kathleen Shaw, *Graphic Designer*
Sue Brosious, *Food Stylist*
Sue Finley, *Food Stylist*
Susan Nielsen, *Production Manager*
Deb Klapperich, *Office Manager*
John W. Kramer, *Director of Sales*

Tony Kubat Photography

Pictured on front cover: Fettuccine Chicken Salad (page 20)

Recipes developed and tested by the Land O'Lakes Test Kitchens.

LAND O LAKES® Collector™ Series is published by Russ Moore & Associates, Inc., 4151 Knob Drive, St. Paul, MN 55122, 612-452-0571. Direct correspondence to Attention: Publisher, 4151 Knob Drive, St. Paul, MN 55122.

PRINTED IN USA

Introduction

Pasta!

We're in love with all things Italian, and pasta leads the list. This second volume in the LAND O LAKES® Collector™ Series salutes the food America has adopted as a mealtime favorite.

These family-pleasing recipes celebrate soups, salads both light and hearty, side dishes to complement many a meal, and entrees that'll have 'em coming back for seconds.

After thorough testing by professional home economists in our Test Kitchens, each recipe comes to you in an easy-to-read, easy-to-follow format that suits the needs of modern cooks. And, of course, we've also included the nutritional information so important in our lives today, along with serving hints.

True to our homespun roots, these recipes recreate the traditional dishes we relish as classic comfort foods like Homestyle Macaroni & Cheese. There are also lots of inventive new creations to tempt modern tastebuds such as Tomato Basil Salad With Mozzarella.

And because today's cooks lead busy lives, there are plenty of dishes that are quick and simple to prepare, including Shrimp Pasta Toss and Quick Tortellini—along with many that appeal to the health-conscious diner, too.

Just serve with love and laughter, the Italian way!

Table of Contents

Popular Kitchen Herb Chart

Used appropriately, herbs can transform a simple dish into a delightful experience of savory, spicy, tangy and piquant flavors.

Basil: *its fresh leaf has a sweet, clovelike spiciness that increases with cooking. Basil combines well with garlic, tomatoes and mushrooms, which makes it an Italian favorite.*

Bay Leaf: *frequently used to make bouquet garnish, marinades, stocks, pates, stuffing and curries. Bay is one herb that is better dried than fresh. Added at the beginning of cooking, the leaf is removed before serving.*

Chives: *chopped and sprinkled on at the end of cooking, chives add a mild onion flavor to soups, salads, chicken, potatoes and more. Blend with butter, cream cheeese, sour cream and sauces. Chives freeze well but are poor dried.*

Cilanto (coriander): *these leaves have a spicy, lemony, pungent flavor that balances perfectly with hot, spicy foods. The potency decreases with cooking. Coriander seeds add an aromatic lift to chutney, curries and vegetables.*

Dill: *the spicy, lemony taste of dill is totally unique. Whole seeds are added to pickles, potato salads, soups and salmon. The leaves enhance both cold and hot sauces, vegetable dips, salads and fish.*

Mint: *has a clean, sharp bite and can be used individually or blended. It adds a refreshing twist to salads and vegetables. It also blends smoothly with chocolate in cakes and desserts. The dainty, delicate leaves are ideal for garnishing.*

Marjoram: *the mild, savory flavor is suitable for tomato dishes, pastas, poultry, meat, fish and vegetables. This herb dries well but is best when added toward the end of cooking.*

Oregano: *has a zesty flavor slightly stronger than marjoram. Its aromatic appeal is a favorite in Italian dishes like pizza, spaghetti and lasagna. It also enhances salads, meat and egg dishes.*

Parsley: *one of the most popular kitchen herbs. Its bright green leaves and mild taste enhance the flavor of other foods and herbs. Use in soups, sauces, salads, dressings, egg dishes and more. Flat leafed Italian parsley and curly parsley both make colorful garnishes.*

Gemelli
Cavatelli
Fusilli
Extra Wide Egg Noodles
Egg Noodles
Angel Hair Pasta
Wagon Wheels
Rigatoni
Vermicelli
Bow-tie Pasta
Mini Lasagna Noodles
Spaghetti
Lasagna
Fettuccine

Pasta Assortment

Pasta comes in almost as many shapes and sizes as there are occasions to enjoy them. Pictured here are a few varieties. Cooking times vary.

Homemade Pasta

Homemade pasta can be made with or without a pasta machine or food processor.

Preparation time: 1 hour • Standing time: 20 minutes • Cooking time: 3 minutes (pictured)

2 to 2 1/3 cups all-purpose flour
1/8 teaspoon salt
1/3 cup water
2 eggs
1 teaspoon olive or vegetable oil

3 quarts (12 cups) water
1 teaspoon salt

In large bowl combine 2 cups flour and 1/8 teaspoon salt. In small bowl, with fork, beat together 1/3 cup water, eggs and oil. Stir egg mixture into flour until dough forms. Turn dough onto floured surface. Knead, sprinkling with remaining 1/3 cup flour as needed to prevent sticking, until dough is smooth and elastic (8 to 10 minutes). Divide dough into quarters. On lightly floured surface roll each quarter into 12-inch square, about 1/16-inch thick. Very lightly sprinkle each square with flour. Let stand 20 minutes. Cut as desired (thin strips, wide strips, squares, etc.).* To cook pasta, in Dutch oven bring 3 quarts water and 1 teaspoon salt to a full boil. Slowly add desired amount of pasta. Cook in boiling water until tender but still firm (2 to 3 minutes).
YIELD: 1 pound (8 servings).

Food Processor Directions: In food processor bowl with metal blade combine flour and 1/8 teaspoon salt. Add eggs and oil. Process with on/off pulses until dough resembles coarse crumbs (30 to 40 seconds). Slowly add water through feed tube while processor is running. Process until dough pulls away from sides of bowl (1 to 2 minutes). If dough is sticky, add 1 tablespoon at a time of remaining 1/3 cup flour, processing with on/off pulses until flour is incorporated into dough. Divide dough into quarters. Continue as directed above.

Pasta Machine Directions: Prepare, knead and divide dough as directed above. Pass each quarter of dough through pasta machine according to manufactures' directions until pasta is about 1/16-inch thick. Continue as directed above.

*At this point, pasta can be dried for about 1 hour, then stored in an airtight container and refrigerated for up to 3 days. Or dry pasta for about 1 hour, seal in freezer bags or freezer container and store in freezer up to 8 months.

Nutrition Information (1 serving): Calorie 140, Protein 5g; Carbohydrate 24g; Fat 2g; Cholesterol 55mg; Sodium 50mg.

COLAVITA

Salads

No wonder everyone loves pasta salads, from the folks around the table to the cook behind the stove: They're easy to assemble, either at the last moment or to accommodate do-ahead demands. They make such a tasty and attractive way to please family and friends. And they're so versatile—the welcome answer to your meal routines.

Grilled Oriental Chicken Pasta Salad

Grilled chicken breasts top a mixture of Oriental vegetables and noodles.

Preparation time: 40 minutes • Grilling time: 18 minutes *(pictured on page 10)*

Chicken

2 (12 ounces each) whole boneless chicken breasts, skinned, halved

2 tablespoons soy sauce

2 (3 ounce) packages Oriental flavor ramen noodle soup

Dressing

1/3 cup vegetable oil

1/3 cup rice vinegar or white wine vinegar

1 seasoning packet from soup mix

3/4 teaspoon ginger

3/4 teaspoon finely chopped fresh garlic

Salad

1 cup pea pods, remove tips and strings, cut in half

1/2 cup chopped green onions

2 medium (1 cup) carrots, cut into very thin 2-inch julienne strips

1/4 cup salted cashews

Prepare grill placing coals to one side; heat until coals are ash white. Make aluminum foil drip pan; place opposite coals. Brush chicken with soy sauce. Place chicken on grill over drip pan. Grill, turning chicken over after half the time, until chicken is fork tender (14 to 18 minutes). Meanwhile, in 2-quart saucepan cook both packages of noodle soup according to package directions using only 1 seasoning packet; drain. Meanwhile, in jar with tight fitting lid, combine all dressing ingredients; shake well. In large bowl toss together noodles and all salad ingredients except cashews; toss gently with dressing. Slice each chicken breast half crosswise into 1-inch pieces; do not separate. To serve, divide salad among 4 plates. Place one chicken breast half on top of each salad. Sprinkle with cashews.

YIELD: 4 servings.

Nutrition Information (1 serving): Calories 580; Protein 35g; Carbohydrate 37g; Fat 32g; Cholesterol 85mg; Sodium 1480mg.

Macaroni & Cheese Salad

A crunchy topping of cheese, bacon and nuts makes this macaroni and cheese salad extra special.

Preparation time: 30 minutes • Chilling time: 2 hours

Salad

5 ounces (1 1/2 cups) uncooked dried rotini (corkscrew or pasta twists)
1 1/2 cups (6 ounces) LAND O LAKES® Shredded Cheddar Cheese
1 1/4 cups mayonnaise
1/2 cup LAND O LAKES® Light Sour Cream or dairy sour cream
1/4 cup chopped celery
1/4 cup chopped green onions
1/4 cup chopped green pepper
1/4 cup milk
1 teaspoon sugar
1/2 teaspoon salt
1/8 teaspoon pepper
2 teaspoons prepared mustard

Topping

1/2 cup (2 ounces) LAND O LAKES® Shredded Cheddar Cheese
1/2 cup walnuts, coarsely chopped
4 slices crisply cooked bacon, crumbled

Cook rotini according to package directions. Rinse with cold water; drain. In large bowl combine rotini and all remaining salad ingredients. Cover; refrigerate at least 2 hours. Just before serving, in small bowl combine all topping ingredients; sprinkle over salad. **YIELD:** 6 servings.

Nutrition Information (1 serving): Calories 540; Protein 17g; Carbohydrate 35g; Fat 38g; Cholesterol 60mg; Sodium 870mg.

Crab & Pasta Salad

This delightful salad makes enough to serve a crowd.

Preparation time: 30 minutes • Chilling time: 2 hours (pictured)

Salad

1 (16 ounce) package uncooked dried rosamarina pasta (orzo)*
2 cups small broccoli flowerets
4 medium (2 cups) carrots, thinly sliced
2 stalks (1 cup) celery, coarsely chopped
3/4 cup chopped red onion
2 (8 ounce) packages imitation crab legs (surimi), cut into 1/2-inch pieces

Dressing

1 (16 ounce) carton (2 cups) LAND O LAKES® Light Sour Cream or dairy sour cream
2 (8 ounce) cartons (2 cups) lowfat plain yogurt
2 to 3 tablespoons chopped fresh thyme leaves**
1 teaspoon salt
1/2 teaspoon pepper

Cook pasta according to package directions. Rinse pasta with cold water; drain. In very large bowl combine pasta and all remaining salad ingredients. In medium bowl stir together all dressing ingredients. Gently stir dressing into salad. Cover; refrigerate at least 2 hours. **YIELD:** 16 servings.

* 2 (7 ounce) packages uncooked dried pasta rings can be substituted for 1 (16 ounce) package uncooked dried rosamarina pasta (orzo).

** 2 teaspoons dried thyme leaves can be substituted for 2 to 3 tablespoons chopped fresh thyme leaves.

Nutrition Information (1 serving); Calories 190; Protein 11g; Carbohydrate 31g; Fat 3g; Cholesterol 15mg; Sodium 230mg.

Peppery Pasta Salad

This one-bowl salad gets a burst of flavor from jalapeno cheese.

Preparation time: 30 minutes • Chilling time: 2 hours (pictured)

4 ounces (2 cups) uncooked dried rotini (corkscrew or pasta twists)
1 slice (1/2-inch thick) cooked turkey or ham (8 to 10 ounces), cubed 1/2-inch
6 ounces LAND O LAKES® Jalapeno Pasteurized Process Cheese Food, cubed 1/2-inch
12 cherry tomatoes, halved
1/2 medium green pepper, cut into strips
1/2 medium red pepper, cut into strips
2/3 cup creamy Italian dressing

Cook rotini according to package directions. Rinse with cold water; drain. In large bowl combine rotini and all remaining ingredients until well coated. Cover; refrigerate at least 2 hours. **YIELD:** 6 servings.

Nutrition Information (1 serving): Calories 330; Protein 19g; Carbohydrate 19g; Fat 18g; Cholesterol 50mg; Sodium 620mg.

Italian Herb Pasta Salad

Using purchased deli marinated vegetable salad makes this recipe extra easy.

Preparation time: 20 minutes • Chilling time: 1 hour

3 ounces (1 cup) uncooked dried radiatore (pasta nuggets)
2 cups (1 pint) deli marinated vegetable salad
1 cup cherry tomatoes, halved
8 ounces (2 cups) LAND O LAKES® Mozzarella or Cheddar Cheese, cubed 1/2-inch
4 ounces (1 cup) hard salami, cubed 1/2-inch

Italian dressing

Cook radiatore according to package directions. Rinse with cold water; drain. In large bowl combine radiatore and all remaining ingredients except dressing. Gently stir in enough dressing to coat. Cover; refrigerate at least 1 hour. **YIELD:** 8 servings.

Nutrition Information (1 serving): Calories 360; Protein 12g; Carbohydrate 14g; Fat 29g; Cholesterol 25mg; Sodium 490mg.

Ham & Cheese Pasta Toss

Prepare this easy salad the night before as a quick next-day supper.

Preparation time: 30 minutes • Chilling time: 2 hours

Salad

6 ounces (2 cups) uncooked dried radiatore (pasta nuggets) or rotini (corkscrew or pasta twists)
1/4 cup sliced green onions
8 ounces (2 cups) LAND O LAKES® Cheddar or Colby Cheese, cubed 1/2-inch
4 ounces (about 30) fresh pea pods, remove tips and strings
1 slice (1/2-inch thick) cooked ham (8 ounces), cut into julienne strips

Dressing

3/4 cup mayonnaise
1/2 cup prepared honey mustard salad dressing

Cook radiatore according to package directions. Rinse with cold water; drain. In large bowl combine pasta and all remaining salad ingredients. In small bowl stir together dressing ingredients. Gently stir dressing into salad. Cover; refrigerate at least 2 hours. **YIELD:** 6 servings.

Nutrition Information (1 serving): Calories 610; Protein 22g; Carbohydrate 28g; Fat 45g; Cholesterol 90mg; Sodium 990mg.

Fettuccine Chicken Salad

A colorful mix of fresh vegetables, chicken and fettuccine makes this a hearty main dish salad.

Preparation time: 45 minutes (pictured on cover and page 21)

Dressing

2/3 cup vegetable oil
1/2 cup white wine vinegar
1 teaspoon dried basil leaves
1 teaspoon dried oregano leaves
1 teaspoon finely chopped fresh garlic
1 teaspoon salt
1/2 teaspoon pepper

Salad

6 ounces uncooked dried fettuccine, broken into thirds
2 1/2 cups cubed 1-inch cooked chicken <u>or</u> turkey
2 cups broccoli flowerets
2 medium (1 cup) carrots, sliced 1/4-inch
1/2 medium red onion, sliced into 1/8-inch rings
1 cup cherry tomatoes, halved

In jar with tight-fitting lid combine all dressing ingredients; shake well. Set aside. Cook fettuccine according to package directions. Rinse with cold water; drain. In large bowl combine fettuccine and all remaining salad ingredients. Gently stir in dressing. YIELD: 6 servings.

Nutrition Information (1 serving): Calories 450; Protein 22g; Carbohydrate 27g; Fat 29g; Cholesterol 50mg; Sodium 420mg.

Layered Rainbow Pasta Salad

Sun-kissed tomato and artichoke hearts combine with an array of colorful ingredients in this main dish salad.

Preparation time: 45 minutes

4 ounces (1 1/4 cups) uncooked dried rotini (corkscrew or pasta twists)
4 cups torn leaf lettuce
3 cups (12 ounces) LAND O LAKES® Shredded Cheddar Cheese
1 large ripe tomato, sliced 1/4-inch, slices halved
1 (14 ounce) can artichoke hearts, drained, cut into 1-inch pieces
12 slices crisply cooked bacon, crumbled

2 slices crisply cooked bacon
Italian dressing

Cook rotini according to package directions. Rinse with cold water; drain. In large clear salad bowl layer 2 cups torn lettuce, 1 1/2 cups cheese, tomato, pasta, 2 cups torn lettuce, artichoke hearts, crumbled bacon and remaining cheese. Garnish top with 2 bacon slices; serve with Italian dressing. **YIELD:** 8 servings.

Nutrition Information (1 serving): Calories 400; Protein 18g; Carbohydrate 19g; Fat 29g; Cholesterol 55mg; Sodium 630mg.

Fresh Tuna & Pasta Salad

Fresh poached tuna is tossed with pasta and vegetables in this main dish salad.

Preparation time: 30 minutes • Cooking time: 20 minutes • Chilling time: 1 hour

Tuna

1/2 cup water
1/2 lemon, sliced
1/2 medium onion, sliced
1 pound fresh tuna steak, skinned*
4 1/2 ounces (1 1/2 cups) uncooked dried radiatore (pasta nuggets) <u>or</u> rotini (corkscrew <u>or</u> pasta twists)

Salad

1 cup (3 ounces) pea pods, remove tips and strings, cut in half**
1/2 cup sliced 1/4-inch celery
1/2 cup coarsely chopped red, yellow <u>or</u> green pepper
1/4 cup chopped onion

Dressing

1/2 cup mayonnaise
1/4 cup lemon juice
2 teaspoons chopped fresh thyme leaves***
1/8 teaspoon salt
1/8 teaspoon pepper

In 2-quart saucepan bring water, lemon and sliced onion to a full boil; add tuna steak. Cover; cook over medium heat until tuna flakes with a fork (15 to 20 minutes). Drain; cool until easy to handle. Flake tuna into bite-size pieces. Meanwhile, cook radiatore according to package directions. Rinse with cold water; drain. In large bowl toss together flaked tuna, radiatore and all remaining salad ingredients. In small bowl, using wire whisk, stir together all dressing ingredients. Gently stir dressing into salad. Cover; refrigerate at least 1 hour. **YIELD:** 6 servings.

* 2 (6 1/8 ounce) cans white tuna packed in water can be substituted for cooked tuna steak. Omit water, lemon and sliced onion.

**1/2 cup fresh peas or frozen peas, thawed, drained, can be substituted for 1 cup (3 ounces) pea pods, remove tips and strings, cut in half.

***1/2 teaspoon dried thyme leaves can be substituted for 2 teaspoons chopped fresh thyme leaves.

Nutrition Information (1 serving): Calories 320; Protein 19g; Carbohydrate 20g; Fat 18g; Cholesterol 35mg; Sodium 190mg.

Dill N' Salmon Pasta Salad

A light, refreshing summertime supper. Serve this pasta salad with multi-grain bread and fresh fruit.

Preparation time: 30 minutes • Chilling time: 1 hour (pictured)

7 ounces (2 1/4 cups) uncooked dried rotini (corkscrew or pasta twists)
1/3 cup cubed 1/2-inch red pepper
1/3 cup vegetable oil
1/4 cup lemon juice
8 ounces salmon fillet, cooked, chunked
8 ounces (2 cups) LAND O LAKES® Cheddar Cheese, cubed 1/2-inch
1 teaspoon dried dill weed
1/2 teaspoon garlic salt
2 tablespoons sliced green onions
Salt and pepper

Cook rotini according to package directions. Rinse with cold water; drain. In large bowl gently stir together all ingredients; season with salt and pepper to taste. Cover; refrigerate at least 1 hour.
YIELD: 6 servings.

TIP: To cook salmon, place in 10-inch skillet; cover with water. Cook over medium heat until salmon flakes with a fork (12 to 15 minutes).

Nutrition Information (1 serving): Calories 440; Protein 21g; Carbohydrate 25g; Fat 28g; Cholesterol 60mg; Sodium 410mg.

Italian Pasta N' Cheese Salad

Two popular Italian herbs, oregano and basil, add extra zest to this pasta and cheese salad.

Preparation time: 30 minutes • Chilling time: 2 hours

Dressing

1/4 cup vegetable oil
1/4 cup cider vinegar
2 teaspoons sugar
1 teaspoon dried basil leaves
1 teaspoon dried oregano leaves
1/4 teaspoon pepper

Salad

6 ounces (2 cups) uncooked dried rotini (corkscrew or pasta twists)
1 1/2 cups broccoli flowerets
8 ounces (2 cups) LAND O LAKES® Mozzarella Cheese, cubed 1/2-inch
2 medium (1 1/2 cups) zucchini, sliced 1/4-inch
1/2 medium (1/2 cup) red onion rings
1 medium red pepper, cut into strips

In jar with tight fitting lid combine all dressing ingredients; shake well. Set aside. Cook rotini according to package directions. Rinse with cold water; drain. In large bowl combine rotini and all remaining salad ingredients. Gently stir dressing into salad. Cover; refrigerate at least 2 hours. **YIELD:** 8 servings.

Nutrition Information (1 serving): Calories 230; Protein 11g; Carbohydrate 21g; Fat 12g; Cholesterol 15mg; Sodium 160mg.

Shrimp & Pasta In Green Peppers

This shrimp and grape pasta salad is served in green pepper halves.

Preparation time: 45 minutes • Cooking time: 4 minutes • Chilling time: 2 hours

Salad

3 1/2 ounces (1/2 cup) uncooked dried rosamarina pasta (orzo)
6 cups water
1 tablespoon mixed pickling spice, optional
1 pound fresh or frozen raw medium shrimp, shelled, deveined, rinsed
1/2 cup sliced 1/2-inch celery
1/2 cup halved red seedless grapes
1/4 cup chopped green pepper
2 tablespoons finely chopped onion
2 large green peppers, cut in half crosswise, seeded

Dressing

1/2 cup plain yogurt
1/4 cup mayonnaise
1 teaspoon chopped fresh marjoram leaves*
1/4 teaspoon grated lemon peel
1/4 teaspoon salt
1/8 teaspoon pepper

Cook pasta according to package directions. Rinse with cold water; drain. Set aside. Meanwhile, in 3-quart saucepan bring water to a full boil; add pickling spice. Add shrimp. Cook over high heat until shrimp just turn pink (3 to 4 minutes). Drain; rinse with cold water. Remove pickling spice. In large bowl combine pasta, shrimp and all remaining salad ingredients except halved green peppers. In small bowl, with wire whisk, stir together all dressing ingredients. Gently stir dressing into salad. Cover; refrigerate at least 2 hours. To serve, spoon salad mixture into green pepper halves. **YIELD:** 4 servings.

*1/4 teaspoon dried marjoram leaves can be substituted for 1 teaspoon chopped fresh marjoram leaves.

Nutrition Information (1 serving):Calories 330; Protein 23g; Carbohydrate 30g; Fat 14g; Cholesterol 140mg; Sodium 380mg.

Pasta With Mixed Salad Greens & Raspberries

Crisp salad greens and pasta are served with a light vinaigrette dressing.

Preparation time: 30 minutes (pictured)

2 ounces (1/2 cup) uncooked dried cavatelli pasta or medium pasta shells

Dressing

1/3 cup olive or vegetable oil
1/4 cup raspberry vinegar or white wine vinegar
1/4 teaspoon finely chopped fresh garlic
1/8 teaspoon salt
1/8 teaspoon coarsely ground pepper

Salad

3 cups mixed salad greens (romaine lettuce, Bibb lettuce, curly endive, radicchio, red cabbage, etc.)
1/2 cup fresh or frozen no sugar added raspberries
1 tablespoon chopped fresh mint leaves

Cook pasta according to package directions. Rinse with cold water; drain. Meanwhile, in jar with tight fitting lid combine all dressing ingredients; shake well. Just before serving, in large bowl combine pasta and all salad ingredients. Gently stir in 1/4 cup dressing. Serve remaining dressing with salad. **YIELD:** 6 servings.

TIP: Mixed or fancy mixed salad greens can be found in your grocer's produce section.

Nutrition Information (1 serving): Calories 150; Protein 2g; Carbohydrate 9g; Fat 12g; Cholesterol 0mg; Sodium 50mg.

Spinach & Pasta Salad

A dressing made with sour cream and orange juice adds a refreshing taste to this salad.

Preparation time: 45 minutes

4 ounces (1 1/2 cups) uncooked dried bow tie pasta

Dressing

1/2 cup LAND O LAKES® Light Sour Cream <u>or</u> dairy sour cream
1/4 cup orange juice
2 tablespoons chopped green onions
1 teaspoon grated orange peel
1 teaspoon sugar

Salad

3 cups lightly packed torn fresh spinach leaves
1/4 cup pine nuts, toasted
6 slices crisply cooked bacon, crumbled
1 medium orange, pared, sectioned

Cook pasta according to package directions. Rinse with cold water; drain. Meanwhile, in small bowl, with wire whisk, stir together all dressing ingredients. To serve, in large bowl combine pasta and all salad ingredients. Gently stir in <u>1/2 cup</u> dressing. Serve remaining dressing with salad. **YIELD:** 6 servings.

TIP: To toast pine nuts, spread nuts on cookie sheet. Bake at 350°, stirring after half the time, for 3 to 6 minutes or until light golden brown.

Nutrition Information (1 serving): Calories 180; Protein 8g; Carbohydrate 22g; Fat 8g; Cholesterol 10mg; Sodium 140mg.

Honeyed Fruit & Pasta Salad

A touch of honey sweetens this unique pasta, vegetable & fruit salad.

Preparation time: 20 minutes • Chilling time: 3 hours

9 ounces (2 cups) fresh tortellini*
2 cups broccoli flowerets
1/4 cup honey
8 ounces (2 cups) cubed 1/2-inch LAND O LAKES® Cheddar Cheese
1 (15 1/4 ounce) can pineapple chunks in pineapple juice, drained
1 (11 ounce) can mandarin orange segments, drained
1/2 teaspoon celery seed

Cook tortellini according to package directions. Rinse with cold water; drain. In large bowl stir together tortellini and all remaining ingredients. Cover; refrigerate at least 3 hours. **YIELD:** 8 servings.

* 3 1/2 ounces (3/4 cup) uncooked dried tortellini can be substituted for 9 ounces (2 cups) fresh tortellini.

Nutrition Information (1 serving): Calories 270; Protein 12g; Carbohydrate 35g; Fat 10g; Cholesterol 55mg; Sodium 190mg.

Sunshine Pasta Salad

Prepare this lemon pasta salad when tomatoes are garden-ripe and bursting with flavor.

Preparation time: 30 minutes (pictured)

4 ounces (1 1/4 cups) uncooked dried rotini (corkscrew or pasta twists)
1 (6 ounce) jar marinated artichoke hearts, quartered, reserve marinade
1/2 cup chopped fresh parsley
1 medium (1 cup) cucumber, sliced 1/8-inch
1/2 teaspoon salt
1/2 teaspoon dried dill weed
1/4 teaspoon pepper
1 tablespoon grated lemon peel
2 tablespoons lemon juice
4 medium ripe tomatoes

Cook rotini according to package directions. Rinse with cold water; drain. In large bowl combine rotini, artichokes, reserved marinade and all remaining ingredients except tomatoes. Remove stems from tomatoes; cut each tomato into 4 wedges, leaving 1/2-inch base to keep tomato intact. Serve 1 cup pasta over each tomato. **YIELD:** 4 servings.

Nutrition Information (1 serving): Calories220; Protein 6g; Carbohydrate 33g; Fat 8g; Cholestrol 0mg; Sodium 430mg.

Tortellini, Broccoli & Blue Cheese Salad

Fresh summer savory complements blue cheese in this robust tortellini salad.

Preparation time: 30 minutes

9 ounces (2 cups) uncooked fresh cheese tortellini*
1 1/2 cups small broccoli flowerets

Dressing

1/2 cup olive or vegetable oil
1/3 cup red wine vinegar or cider vinegar
1/8 teaspoon salt
1/8 teaspoon pepper

Salad

1/2 medium red onion, sliced, separated into rings
1/3 cup crumbled blue cheese
1 tablespoon chopped fresh summer savory leaves**

Leaf lettuce

Cook tortellini according to package directions adding broccoli to tortellini during last 1 minute of cooking time. Rinse with cold water; drain. Meanwhile, in jar with tight fitting lid combine all dressing ingredients; shake well. To serve, in medium bowl combine tortellini and all salad ingredients. Gently stir in dressing. Cover; refrigerate until ready to serve. Serve on lettuce-lined plates. **YIELD:** 6 servings.

*3 1/2 ounces (3/4 cup) uncooked dried cheese tortellini can be substituted for 9 ounces uncooked fresh cheese tortellini.

**1/2 teaspoon dried summer savory leaves can be substituted for 1 tablespoon chopped fresh summer savory leaves.

Nutrition Information (1 serving): Calories 330; Protein 9g; Carbohydrate 24g; Fat 22g; Cholesterol 30mg; Sodium 350mg.

Tomato Basil Salad With Mozzarella

Favorite Italian flavors are tossed together in this spaghetti salad.

Preparation time: 30 minutes

Pasta

3 ounces uncooked dried angel hair pasta (very thin spaghetti), broken into thirds

Dressing

1/4 cup olive or vegetable oil
1/4 cup red wine vinegar or cider vinegar
2 teaspoons sugar
1/8 teaspoon salt
1/8 teaspoon coarsely ground pepper
1 teaspoon finely chopped fresh garlic

Salad

1/4 cup chopped fresh basil leaves*
4 medium ripe Roma tomatoes, sliced 1/4-inch
4 ounces (1 cup) cubed 1/2-inch LAND O LAKES® Mozzarella Cheese

Leaf lettuce
Fresh basil leaves, if desired

Cook pasta according to package directions. Rinse with cold water; drain. Meanwhile, in jar with tight fitting lid combine all dressing ingredients; shake well. Just before serving, in large bowl combine pasta, basil, tomatoes and Mozzarella cheese. Gently stir in dressing. Place 1 lettuce leaf on each individual serving plate or line large serving plate with lettuce. Arrange salad on plates. Garnish with additional basil leaves. **YIELD:** 6 servings.

*2 teaspoons dried basil leaves can be substituted for 1/4 cup chopped fresh basil leaves.

Nutrition Information (1 serving): Calories 200; Protein 7g; Carbohydrate 15g; Fat 13g; Cholesterol 10mg; Sodium 150mg.

Side Dishes

Tossed with vegetables, stirred into a smooth sauce, or dressed up with herbs or cheese, these side dishes add that satisfying little "extra something" that transforms a mundane dinner into a memorable meal.

Vegetable & Pasta Toss

Fresh garden vegetables bring a homemade taste to this unique dish.

Preparation time: 25 minutes • Cooking time: 4 minutes (pictured on page 36)

6 ounces uncooked dried linguine
2 medium (2 cups) zucchini, sliced 1/4-inch
2 medium (2 cups) summer squash, sliced 1/4-inch
1/4 cup LAND O LAKES® Butter
2 tablespoons chopped fresh dill weed*
1/4 teaspoon salt
1/8 teaspoon pepper
1 teaspoon lemon juice
1/2 pint cherry tomatoes, halved

Freshly grated Parmesan cheese

Cook linguine according to package directions. Rinse with hot water; drain. Meanwhile, in 10-inch skillet bring 1/2 inch water to a full boil; add zucchini and summer squash. Cover; cook over medium high heat until vegetables are crisply tender (3 to 4 minutes). Drain; set aside. In same pan used to prepare linguine melt butter until sizzling; stir in dill, salt, pepper and lemon juice. Remove from heat. Add linguine, cooked vegetables and tomatoes; toss lightly to coat. Serve with Parmesan cheese. **YIELD:** 6 servings.

*2 teaspoons dried dill weed can be substituted for 2 tablespoons fresh dill.

Nutrition Information (1 serving): Calories 190; Protein 5g; Carbohydrate 24g; Fat 8g; Cholesterol 20mg; Sodium 170mg.

Home-Style Macaroni & Cheese

Macaroni with chunks of Cheddar cheese is baked until bubbling for a soothing and satisfying supper.

Preparation time: 15 minutes • Cooking time: 5 minutes • Baking time: 20 minutes

7 ounces (2 cups) uncooked dried elbow macaroni
1/4 cup LAND O LAKES® Butter
3 tablespoons all-purpose flour
2 cups milk
1 (8 ounce) package cream cheese, softened
1/2 teaspoon salt
1/2 teaspoon pepper
2 teaspoons country-style Dijon mustard
8 ounces (2 cups) LAND O LAKES® Cheddar Cheese, cubed 1/2-inch
1 cup fresh bread crumbs
2 tablespoons LAND O LAKES® Butter, melted
2 tablespoons chopped fresh parsley

Heat oven to 400°. Cook macaroni according to package directions. Rinse with hot water; drain. Meanwhile, in 3-quart saucepan melt 1/4 cup butter; stir in flour. Cook over medium heat, stirring occasionally, until smooth and bubbly (1 minute). Add milk, cream cheese, salt, pepper and mustard; continue cooking, stirring occasionally, until sauce is thickened (3 to 4 minutes). Stir in macaroni and cheese. Pour into 2-quart casserole. In small bowl stir together all remaining ingredients; sprinkle over macaroni and cheese. Bake for 15 to 20 minutes or until golden brown and heated through. **YIELD:** 6 servings.

Nutrition Information (1 serving): Calories 580; Protein 20g; Carbohydrate 36g; Fat 40g; Cholesterol 120mg; Sodium 740mg.

Vegetable Medley With Pasta

Ziti pasta comes shaped in long, thin tubes.

Preparation time: 15 minutes • Cooking time: 6 minutes (pictured)

- **4 ounces (1 1/4 cups) uncooked dried ziti pasta**
- **2 tablespoons olive <u>or</u> vegetable oil**
- **2 teaspoons finely chopped fresh garlic**
- **1 (16 ounce) package frozen vegetable mixture (broccoli, red pepper, cauliflower, pearl onions, carrots, etc.)**
- **1/4 cup white wine <u>or</u> chicken broth**
- **1/2 cup freshly grated Parmesan cheese**
- **1/4 cup chopped fresh basil leaves***
- **1/8 teaspoon salt**
- **1/8 teaspoon pepper**

Cook pasta according to package directions. Rinse with hot water; drain. Meanwhile, in 10-inch skillet heat oil; add garlic. Stir in vegetable mixture. Cook over medium high heat, stirring constantly, 1 minute. Reduce heat to medium. Stir in wine. Cover; continue cooking, stirring occasionally, until vegetables are crisply tender (3 to 5 minutes). Place pasta in large bowl; toss with vegetables and all remaining ingredients. **YIELD:** 6 servings.

*1 tablespoon dried basil leaves can be substituted for 1/4 cup chopped fresh basil leaves.

Nutrition Information (1 serving): Calories 170; Protein 7g; Carbohydrate 19g; Fat 7g; Cholesterol 5mg; Sodium 220mg.

Butter Crumb Noodles

Fresh, buttery bread crumbs tossed with egg noodles make an easy family side dish.

Preparation time: 20 minutes • Cooking time: 7 minutes

8 ounces (4 cups) uncooked dried egg noodles
1/3 cup LAND O LAKES® Butter
3 slices whole wheat <u>or</u> white bread
1/4 cup chopped fresh parsley
1/4 to 1/2 teaspoon coarsely ground pepper
1/4 teaspoon salt

Cook egg noodles according to package directions. Rinse with hot water; drain. Meanwhile, place bread in food processor bowl or 5-cup blender container. Process with pulses until coarse crumbs are formed. In 10-inch skillet melt butter until sizzling; add bread crumbs. Cook over medium heat, stirring constantly, until golden brown (5 to 7 minutes). Toss hot cooked noodles with bread crumbs, parsley, pepper and salt. **YIELD:** 6 servings.

TIP: If using a blender, process 1 slice of bread at a time.

Nutrition Information (1 serving): Calories 270; Protein 6g; Carbohydrate 34g; Fat 12g; Cholesterol 65mg; Sodium 260mg.

Buttery Noodles & Herbs

A quick and easy side dish, this pasta is flavored with two favorite herbs.

Preparation time: 20 minutes

8 ounces (4 cups) uncooked dried egg noodles
1/3 cup freshly grated Parmesan cheese
3 tablespoons LAND O LAKES® Butter
1 teaspoon chopped fresh basil leaves*
1 teaspoon chopped fresh oregano leaves**
2 teaspoons lemon juice

Cook noodles according to package directions. Rinse with hot water; drain. Return to saucepan. Stir in all remaining ingredients until well mixed and butter is melted. **YIELD:** 4 servings.

* 1/2 teaspoon dried basil leaves can be substituted for 1 teaspoon chopped fresh basil leaves.

** 1/2 teaspoon dried oregano leaves can be substituted for 1 teaspoon chopped fresh oregano leaves.

Nutrition Information (1 serving): Calories 350; Protein 12g; Carbohydrate 45g; Fat 14g; Cholesterol 90mg; Sodium 250mg.

German Skillet Pasta

This pasta side dish is reminiscent of German potato salad.

Preparation time: 15 minutes • Cooking time: 12 minutes (pictured)

4 1/2 ounces (1 1/4 cups) uncooked dried tri-colored wagon wheel pasta
4 slices bacon, cut into 1-inch pieces
2 tablespoons sugar
1 tablespoon all-purpose flour
1/8 teaspoon salt
1/8 teaspoon pepper
1 tablespoon country-style Dijon mustard
1/3 cup water
1/4 cup vinegar
1/2 cup sliced 1/4-inch celery
1/4 cup chopped onion
1 tablespoon chopped fresh parsley

Cook pasta according to package directions. Rinse with hot water; drain. Meanwhile, in 10-inch skillet cook bacon over medium high heat until crisp (2 to 3 minutes). Reduce heat to medium. Stir in sugar, flour, salt, pepper and mustard. Continue cooking, stirring constantly, 1 minute. Add water and vinegar. Continue cooking, stirring constantly, until mixture just comes to a boil and thickens (2 to 4 minutes). Stir in pasta, celery and onion. Continue cooking, stirring occasionally, until heated through (2 to 4 minutes). Sprinkle with parsley. **YIELD:** 6 servings.

Nutrition Information (1 serving): Calories 130; Protein 4g; Carbohydrate 22g; Fat 3g; Cholesterol 5mg; Sodium 150mg.

Mushrooms, Chevre & Pasta

An interesting assortment of mushrooms and goat cheese makes this pasta more upscale.

Preparation time: 20 minutes • Cooking time: 9 minutes

4 ounces (1 cup) gemelli (double twist pasta) or rotini (corkscrew or pasta twists)
1/4 cup LAND O LAKES® Butter
2 teaspoons finely chopped fresh garlic
4 cups sliced assorted mushrooms (oyster, shitake, morel, button, etc.)
1/4 cup chopped onion
1/2 medium red pepper, cut into thin strips
1 tablespoon chopped fresh parsley
1 tablespoon chopped fresh basil leaves*
1/8 teaspoon salt
1/8 teaspoon pepper
1 (6 ounce) package Chevre cheese (soft white goat cheese)**

Cook gemelli according to package directions. Rinse with hot water; drain. Meanwhile, in 10-inch skillet melt butter until sizzling; stir in garlic. Stir in all remaining ingredients except pasta and Chevre cheese. Cook over medium heat, stirring occasionally, until vegetables are crisply tender (4 to 5 minutes). Stir in Chevre cheese. Continue cooking, stirring constantly, until Chevre cheese is melted (2 to 4 minutes). Toss with hot cooked gemelli. Serve immediately. **YIELD:** 8 servings.

*1 teaspoon dried basil leaves can be substituted for 1 tablespoon chopped fresh basil leaves.

**6 ounces cream cheese, softened, plus 2 teaspoons lemon juice can be substituted for 1 (6 ounce) package Chevre cheese.

Nutrition Information (1 serving): Calories 190; Protein 4g; Carbohydrate 14g; Fat 14g; Cholesterol 40mg; Sodium 160mg.

Poppy Seed Noodles N' Cream

Poppy seed and sour cream bring old world flavor to this quick side dish.

Preparation time: 15 minutes • Cooking time: 2 minutes

8 ounces (4 cups) uncooked extra wide egg noodles
1 (8 ounce) carton (1 cup) LAND O LAKES® Light Sour Cream or dairy sour cream
1/4 cup LAND O LAKES® Butter
2 teaspoons poppy seed
1/2 teaspoon salt

In 3-quart saucepan cook noodles according to package directions. Rinse with hot water; drain. Return to pan; add all remaining ingredients. Cook over medium heat, stirring constantly, until well mixed and heated through (1 to 2 minutes). **YIELD:** 6 servings.

Nutrition Information (1 serving): Calories 270; Protein 7g; Carbohydrate 34g; Fat 12g; Cholesterol 70mg; Sodium 290mg.

Mini Lasagna With Fresh Tomatoes

This pleasing recipe combines ripe Roma tomatoes, fresh herbs and a unique pasta.

Preparation time: 25 minutes • Cooking time: 6 minutes (pictured)

4 ounces (1 1/2 cups) uncooked dried mini lasagna noodles or bow tie pasta
2 tablespoons olive or vegetable oil
4 medium (2 cups) ripe Roma tomatoes, seeded, cut into 1-inch pieces*
2 tablespoons chopped fresh basil leaves**
1 tablespoon chopped fresh oregano leaves***
1/8 teaspoon salt
1/8 teaspoon pepper
2 teaspoons finely chopped fresh garlic
1/3 cup freshly grated Parmesan cheese

Cook noodles according to package directions. Rinse with hot water; drain. Meanwhile, in 10-inch skillet heat oil; stir in tomatoes, basil, oregano, salt, pepper and garlic. Cook over medium high heat, stirring constantly, until heated through (2 to 3 minutes). Add noodles. Continue cooking, stirring occasionally, until flavors are blended (2 to 3 minutes). Toss with Parmesan cheese. Serve immediately. **YIELD:** 6 servings.

*2 medium (2 cups) ripe tomatoes, seeded, cut into 1-inch pieces, can be substituted for 4 medium (2 cups) ripe Roma tomatoes, seeded, cut into 1-inch pieces.

**2 teaspoons dried basil leaves can be substituted for 2 tablespoons chopped fresh basil leaves.

***1 teaspoon dried oregano leaves can be substituted for 1 tablespoon chopped fresh oregano leaves.

Nutrition Information (1 serving): Calories 150; Protein 5g; Carbohydrate 17g; Fat 7g; Cholesterol 5mg; Sodium 150mg.

Rigatoni With Eggplant & Parmesan Cheese

This pasta is tossed with eggplant and garden-ripened tomatoes.

Preparation time: 25 minutes • Cooking time: 17 minutes

8 ounces (3 cups) uncooked dried rigatoni
8 slices bacon, cut into 1-inch pieces
1 medium eggplant, sliced 1/4-inch, cut in half
1/2 teaspoon finely chopped fresh garlic
2 cups (8 ounces) fresh mushrooms, halved
2 medium (2 cups) ripe tomatoes, cut into 1-inch pieces
1/2 teaspoon coarsely ground pepper
1/4 teaspoon salt
1/8 teaspoon ground red pepper, if desired
1 tablespoon olive or vegetable oil
1/2 cup chopped fresh parsley

2 ounces freshly shaved or grated Parmesan cheese

Cook rigatoni according to package directions. Rinse with hot water; drain. Meanwhile, in Dutch oven cook bacon, eggplant and garlic over medium high heat, stirring occasionally, until bacon is browned (6 to 8 minutes). Reduce heat to medium. Stir in all remaining ingredients except rigatoni, parsley and Parmesan cheese. Cook, stirring occasionally, until mushrooms are tender (3 to 4 minutes). Add rigatoni and parsley. Continue cooking, stirring occasionally, until rigatoni is heated through (3 to 5 minutes). Top with shavings of Parmesan cheese. **YIELD:** 6 servings.

Nutrition Information (1 serving): Calories 500; Protein 20g; Carbohydrate 79g; Fat 11g; Cholesterol 15mg; Sodium 410mg.

Florentine Mostaccioli

Serve this pasta dish with broiled hamburgers or steak.

Preparation time: 15 minutes • Cooking time: 16 minutes

9 ounces (3 cups) uncooked dried mostaccioli or rigatoni*
3 tablespoons LAND O LAKES® Butter
1/3 cup chopped onion
3 tablespoons all-purpose flour
1/4 teaspoon salt
1/8 teaspoon nutmeg
1/8 teaspoon pepper
1 1/2 cups half-and-half
1/2 cup freshly grated Parmesan cheese
1 (10 ounce) package frozen chopped spinach, thawed, well drained

Cook mostaccioli according to package directions. Rinse with hot water; drain. Meanwhile, in 3-quart saucepan melt butter until sizzling; add onion. Cook over medium heat, stirring occasionally, until onions are tender (4 to 6 minutes). Stir in flour, salt, nutmeg and pepper. Continue cooking, stirring constantly, until smooth and bubbly (1 minute). Add half-and-half; continue cooking until mixture comes to a full boil (3 to 4 minutes). Stir in Parmesan cheese and spinach. Stir in mostaccioli; reduce heat to low. Continue cooking, stirring occasionally, until heated through (4 to 5 minutes). **YIELD:** 6 servings.

* 9 ounces (3 cups) uncooked dried medium pasta shells can be substituted for 9 ounces (3 cups) uncooked dried mostaccioli.

Nutrition Information (1 serving): Calories 360; Protein 13g; Carbohydrate 41g; Fat 16g; Cholesterol 45mg; Sodium 360mg.

Pasta With Artichoke Hearts

A rich, tangy pasta sauce with artichoke hearts and red pepper.

Preparation time: 20 minutes • Cooking time: 13 minutes (pictured)

- 8 ounces uncooked dried spinach fettuccine
- 1 cup mayonnaise
- 1 1/2 cups milk
- 1 tablespoon all-purpose flour
- 1 cup (4 ounces) LAND O LAKES® Shredded Mozzarella Cheese
- 1/2 cup chopped fresh parsley
- 1/4 cup freshly grated Parmesan cheese
- 1 medium (1 cup) red pepper, coarsely chopped
- 1 (14 ounce) can artichoke hearts, drained, quartered
- 1/2 teaspoon coarsely ground pepper
- 1/8 teaspoon ground red pepper
- 1 teaspoon finely chopped fresh garlic

Cook fettuccine according to package directions. Rinse with hot water; drain. Meanwhile, in 10-inch skillet, with wire whisk, stir together mayonnaise, milk and flour. Cook over medium heat, stirring occasionally, until smooth (2 to 3 minutes). Add all remaining ingredients except fettuccine. Continue cooking, stirring occasionally, until mixture comes to a full boil (6 to 10 minutes). Serve over hot cooked fettuccine. **YIELD:** 6 servings.

Nutrition Information (1 serving): Calories 540; Protein 16g; Carbohydrate 40g; Fat 36g; Cholesterol 40mg; Sodium 450mg.

Fettuccine With Spinach Cream Sauce

Butter and cream make this delicate spinach sauce rich in flavor.

Preparation time: 20 minutes • Cooking time: 12 minutes

8 ounces uncooked dried fettuccine
3 tablespoons LAND O LAKES® Butter
1 cup sliced 1/4-inch fresh mushrooms
1 tablespoon all-purpose flour
1/4 cup freshly grated Parmesan cheese
1 1/2 cups half-and-half
1 (10 ounce) package frozen chopped spinach, thawed, drained
15 cherry tomatoes, halved
1 teaspoon dried basil leaves
1/2 teaspoon salt
1/4 teaspoon pepper

Cook fettuccine according to package directions. Rinse with hot water; drain. Meanwhile, in 10-inch skillet melt butter until sizzling; add mushrooms. Cook over medium heat, stirring occasionally, until mushrooms are tender (2 to 3 minutes). Stir in flour until smooth and bubbly (1 minute). Stir in all remaining ingredients. Continue cooking, stirring occasionally, until heated through (6 to 8 minutes). Serve over hot fettuccine. **YIELD:** 4 servings.

Nutrition Information (1 serving): Calories 460; Protein 15g; Carbohydrate 52g; Fat 22g; Cholesterol 60mg; Sodium 560mg.

Creamy Vegetables & Fettuccine

A colorful pasta side dish; serve with roast beef and a green salad for a hearty meal.

Preparation time: 20 minutes • Cooking time: 23 minutes

4 medium (2 cups) 1/2-inch carrots, diagonally sliced
6 ounces uncooked dried fettuccine
2 cups broccoli flowerets
6 tablespoons LAND O LAKES® Butter
2 tablespoons all-purpose flour
1/2 teaspoon salt
1/2 teaspoon nutmeg
1 cup milk
1/4 cup freshly grated Parmesan cheese

In 3-quart saucepan bring 8 cups water to a full boil; add carrots and fettuccine. Cook over medium heat 6 minutes. Add broccoli; continue cooking until carrots and broccoli are crisply tender (4 to 5 minutes); rinse with hot water. Drain; set aside. In same saucepan melt butter over medium heat; stir in flour, salt and nutmeg until smooth and bubbly (1 minute). Add milk; cook over medium heat, stirring occasionally, until mixture comes to a full boil (4 to 6 minutes). Boil 1 minute. Stir in fettuccine mixture. Reduce heat to low; continue cooking until heated through (3 to 4 minutes). To serve, sprinkle with Parmesan cheese. **YIELD:** 6 servings.

Nutrition Information (1 serving): Calories 280; Protein 8g; Carbohydrate 30g; Fat 14g; Cholesterol 35mg; Sodium 410mg.

Fettuccine With Asparagus

Crisply tender asparagus and fettuccine are complemented with fresh rosemary.

Preparation time: 20 minutes • Cooking time: 14 minutes (pictured)

2 ounces uncooked dried fettuccine
2 tablespoons olive or vegetable oil
1/4 cup chopped onion
2 teaspoons finely chopped fresh garlic
3/4 pound (18) fresh asparagus spears, trimmed, cut into thirds*
1/2 teaspoon chopped fresh rosemary leaves**
1/8 teaspoon salt
1/8 teaspoon pepper
1/2 cup half-and-half
1/3 cup freshly grated Romano or Parmesan cheese

Cook fettuccine according to package directions. Rinse with hot water; drain. Meanwhile, in 10-inch skillet heat oil; stir in onion and garlic. Cook over medium heat, stirring occasionally, until onion is crisply tender (2 to 3 minutes). Stir in asparagus, rosemary, salt and pepper. Continue cooking, stirring occasionally, until asparagus turns bright green (2 to 3 minutes); cover. Continue cooking, stirring occasionally, until asparagus is crisply tender (5 to 6 minutes). Stir in fettuccine, half-and-half and cheese. Continue cooking, stirring constantly, until heated through (1 to 2 minutes). Serve immediately. **YIELD:** 6 servings.

*1 (9 ounce) package frozen asparagus cuts can be substituted for 3/4 pound (18) fresh asparagus spears, trimmed, cut into thirds.

**1/8 teaspoon crushed dried rosemary leaves can be substituted for 1/2 teaspoon chopped fresh rosemary leaves.

Nutrition Information (1 serving): Calories 140; Protein 6g; Carbohydrate 11g; Fat 9g; Cholesterol 15mg; Sodium 130mg.

Spinach Stuffed Pasta Shells

These pasta shells, stuffed with a unique vegetable mixture, make an interesting main dish accompaniment.

Preparation time: 20 minutes • Cooking time: 7 minutes • Baking time: 16 minutes (pictured)

12 uncooked dried jumbo pasta shells
1/4 cup LAND O LAKES® Butter
2 tablespoons pine nuts or sliced almonds
7 ounces fresh spinach, torn
1 cup sliced 1/4-inch fresh mushrooms
1/2 teaspoon fennel seed
1/2 teaspoon finely chopped fresh garlic
1/2 cup crushed croutons or dried crumbly style herb seasoned stuffing
1/2 cup (2 ounces) LAND O LAKES® Shredded Cheddar Cheese

1 tablespoon LAND O LAKES® Butter, melted
Freshly grated Parmesan cheese
Paprika

Heat oven to 375°. Prepare pasta shells according to package directions. Rinse with hot water; drain. Set aside. In 10-inch skillet melt 1/4 cup butter until sizzling; add pine nuts. Cook over medium heat until toasted (2 to 4 minutes). Add spinach, mushrooms, fennel and garlic; continue cooking until spinach is wilted (2 to 3 minutes). Stir in croutons and Cheddar cheese. Fill each cooked pasta shell with about 2 tablespoons spinach mixture. Place in 9-inch square baking pan. Brush with 1 tablespoon melted butter. Sprinkle with Parmesan cheese and paprika. Cover with aluminum foil; bake 12 minutes. Uncover; continue baking for 2 to 4 minutes or until lightly browned. **YIELD:** 4 servings.

Nutrition Information (1 serving): Calories 470; Protein 15g; Carbohydrate 49g; Fat 24g; Cholesterol 55mg; Sodium 480mg.

Cheddar-Vegetable Stuffed Shells

Cheddar cheese and dill enhance vegetables nestled in pasta shells.

Preparation time: 20 minutes • Baking time: 25 minutes

12 uncooked dried jumbo pasta shells
2 cups frozen vegetable medley
6 ounces (1 1/2 cups) LAND O LAKES® Cheddar <u>or</u> Colby Cheese, cubed 1/2-inch
2 tablespoons LAND O LAKES® Butter, melted
1/2 teaspoon dried dill weed

Heat oven to 350°. Cook shells according to package directions. Rinse with cold water; drain. Dry on paper towel. Place shells in 9-inch square baking pan. In medium bowl stir together vegetables and cheese. Stuff each shell with about <u>1/4 cup</u> mixture. In small bowl stir together melted butter and dill weed; brush over shells. Cover; bake for 20 to 25 minutes or until heated through.
YIELD: 4 servings.

Nutrition Information (1 serving): Calories 450; Protein 19g; Carbohydrate 46g; Fat 21g; Cholesterol 60mg; Sodium 360mg.

Cheese N' Vegetable Linguine

A quick pasta dinner even the kids will love.
An easy shortcut in the recipe lets the carrots and linguine cook together.

Preparation time: 15 minutes • Cooking time: 19 minutes

8 cups water
2 medium (1 cup) carrots, sliced 1/4-inch
7 ounces uncooked dried linguine
2 tablespoons LAND O LAKES® Butter
1 medium (1 cup) zucchini, sliced 1/2-inch, quartered
1/4 cup half-and-half
3 eggs
1/4 teaspoon salt
1 cup (4 ounces) LAND O LAKES® Shredded Mozzarella Cheese
1/2 cup freshly grated Parmesan cheese

Coarsely ground pepper

In 3-quart saucepan bring water to a full boil; add carrots. Cook over medium heat 3 minutes. Add linguine; continue cooking until carrots are crisply tender and linguine is done (8 to 10 minutes). Rinse with hot water; drain. Meanwhile, in 10-inch skillet melt butter until sizzling; add zucchini. Cook over medium heat, stirring occasionally, until zucchini is crisply tender (3 to 4 minutes). In small bowl, with wire whisk, beat together half-and-half, eggs and salt. Add egg mixture, linguine, carrots and cheeses to zucchini; toss gently. Reduce heat to low; continue cooking, stirring constantly, until thickened and cheese is melted (1 to 2 minutes). Serve with pepper. **YIELD:** 4 servings.

Nutrition Information (1 serving): Calories 470; Protein 25g; Carbohydrate 45g; Fat 21g; Cholesterol 250mg; Sodium 660mg.

Skillet Pasta & Vegetables

A new way to use the plentiful zucchini from your garden.

Preparation time: 20 minutes • Cooking time: 9 minutes (pictured)

4 ounces (1 1/2 cups) uncooked dried bow tie pasta*
1/4 cup LAND O LAKES® Butter
1 teaspoon finely chopped fresh garlic
1 medium zucchini, cut into 1/2-inch pieces
1 small eggplant, cut into 1/2-inch pieces
1 medium red onion, cut into eighths
1 teaspoon dried basil leaves
1/2 teaspoon salt
1/2 teaspoon pepper
1 1/2 cups (6 ounces) LAND O LAKES® Shredded Mozzarella Cheese

Cook pasta according to package directions. Rinse with hot water; drain. In 10-inch skillet melt butter until sizzling; stir in garlic. Stir in all remaining ingredients except pasta and cheese. Cook over medium heat, stirring occasionally, until vegetables are crisply tender (4 to 6 minutes). Stir in pasta. Continue cooking, stirring occasionally, until heated through (2 to 3 minutes). Stir in cheese. Serve immediately. **YIELD:** 4 servings.

*4 ounces (2 cups) your favorite uncooked dried pasta can be substituted for 4 ounces (2 cups) uncooked dried bow tie pasta.

Nutrition Information (1 serving): Calories 350; Protein 17g; Carbohydrate 29g; Fat 20g; Cholesterol 55mg; Sodium 610mg.

Main Dishes

Who doesn't like spaghetti? And we're just as wild about fettuccine, rigatoni and lasagna. These popular Italian noodles have become all-American favorites, too. Enjoy them with their traditional seasonings, or wake up your taste buds with some new ideas.

Red Tomato Sauce With Meatballs

Try this traditional family favorite of spaghetti and meatballs.

Preparation time: 45 minutes • Cooking time: 3 hours (pictured on page 64)

Sauce

5 cups water
2 (12 ounce) cans tomato paste
1 medium (1/2 cup) onion, chopped
1 (29 ounce) can tomato puree
3 tablespoons chopped fresh oregano leaves*
1 tablespoon chopped fresh basil leaves**
2 teaspoons sugar
1 teaspoon salt
1 bay leaf
1 teaspoon finely chopped fresh garlic

Meatballs

1/2 cup dry Italian bread crumbs
1/2 cup freshly grated Parmesan cheese
1/2 pound bulk Italian sausage
1/2 pound ground beef
2 eggs
1/4 teaspoon coarsely ground pepper
1/2 teaspoon finely chopped fresh garlic

1 tablespoon olive <u>or</u> vegetable oil

1 (8 ounce) package uncooked dried spaghetti

In Dutch oven combine water and tomato paste. Stir with wire whisk until smooth. Add all remaining sauce ingredients. Cook over medium high heat, stirring occasionally, until sauce just comes to a boil (6 to 8 minutes). Cover; reduce heat to low. Continue cooking, stirring occasionally, until sauce is thickened (1 1/2 to 2 hours). Meanwhile, in large bowl combine all meatball ingredients <u>except</u> oil and spaghetti; mix well. Form into 16 meatballs. In 10-inch skillet heat oil; add meatballs. Cook over medium heat, turning occasionally, until well browned (10 to 12 minutes). Drain meatballs; stir into sauce. Cover loosely; continue cooking over low heat, stirring occasionally, 1 hour. Remove bay leaf. Meanwhile, cook spaghetti according to package directions. Rinse with hot water; drain. Serve sauce and meatballs over hot cooked spaghetti. **YIELD:** 8 servings.

*1 tablespoon dried oregano leaves can be substituted for 3 tablespoons chopped fresh oregano leaves.

**1 teaspoon dried basil leaves can be substituted for 1 tablespoon chopped fresh basil leaves.

TIP: Chopped ripe tomato, sliced mushrooms, sliced black olives or chopped green pepper can be added to sauce during last hour of cooking.

Nutrition Information (1 serving): Calories 410; Protein 21g; Carbohydrate 55g; Fat 14g; Cholesterol 85mg; Sodium 1740mg.

Mustard Cream Pork Chops

Whipping cream is added to the pan drippings of pork chops to make a rich sauce that tastes great over country-style egg noodles.

Preparation time: 30 minutes • Cooking time: 20 minutes

Noodles

1 (12 ounce) package frozen egg noodles*
2 medium (1 cup) onions, chopped
2 medium (1 cup) carrots, sliced 1/4-inch
1/4 teaspoon coarsely ground pepper
1/2 cup chopped fresh parsley

Pork Chops

2 tablespoons LAND O LAKES® Butter
2 tablespoons country-style Dijon mustard
4 (1/2-inch thick) boneless pork chops
1/4 teaspoon coarsely ground pepper
1/8 teaspoon salt
1/2 cup whipping cream

Cook noodles according to package directions with all noodle ingredients except parsley. Rinse with hot water; drain. Meanwhile, in 10-inch skillet melt butter until sizzling; stir in mustard. Place pork chops in skillet; sprinkle with 1/4 teaspoon pepper and salt. Cook over medium heat, turning occasionally, until pork chops are fork tender (15 to 20 minutes). Stir whipping cream into pan juices; spoon over pork chops. Stir parsley into noodles. Serve pork chops and cream sauce over hot cooked noodles. **YIELD**: 4 servings.

*2 cups uncooked dried wide egg noodles can be substituted for 1 (12 ounce) package frozen egg noodles.

Nutrition Information (1 serving): Calories 690; Protein 32g; Carbohydrate 69g; Fat 31g; Cholesterol 200mg; Sodium 430mg.

Green & White Fettuccine

For a fast and delicious dinner, toss fettuccine with ham strips and peas.

Preparation time: 20 minutes • Cooking time: 14 minutes (pictured)

4 ounces uncooked dried fettuccine
4 ounces uncooked dried spinach fettuccine
1/2 cup LAND O LAKES® Butter
1/2 teaspoon finely chopped fresh garlic
1/4 cup chopped fresh parsley
1 cup whipping cream
1 (10 ounce) package frozen peas, thawed
1/4 teaspoon pepper
3/4 cup freshly grated Parmesan cheese
8 ounces cooked ham, cut into julienne strips

Freshly grated Parmesan cheese

In 4-quart saucepan cook both kinds of fettuccine according to package directions. Rinse with hot water; drain. Set aside. In same pan melt butter until sizzling; add garlic. Cook over medium heat, stirring occasionally, until tender (2 to 3 minutes). Stir in parsley, whipping cream, peas and pepper. Continue cooking, stirring occasionally, until heated through (4 to 5 minutes). Stir in both fettuccine, 3/4 cup Parmesan cheese and ham. Continue cooking, stirring occasionally, until heated through and cheese is melted (4 to 6 minutes). Serve with additional Parmesan cheese.
YIELD: 4 servings.

Nutrition Information (1 serving): Calories 720; Protein 31g; Carbohydrate 52g; Fat 43g; Cholesterol 155mg; Sodium 1250mg.

Ham & Broccoli Fettuccine

Two colors of fettuccine are tossed with ham and broccoli for a one-dish supper.

Preparation time: 20 minutes • Cooking time: 16 minutes

4 ounces uncooked dried fettuccine
4 ounces uncooked dried spinach fettuccine
1/2 cup LAND O LAKES® Butter
2 cups broccoli flowerets*
1/2 teaspoon finely chopped fresh garlic
1/4 cup chopped fresh parsley
1 cup whipping cream
1/4 teaspoon pepper
3/4 cup freshly grated Parmesan cheese
4 ounces cubed 1/2-inch cooked ham

Freshly grated Parmesan cheese

In Dutch oven cook fettuccine according to package directions. Rinse with hot water; drain. Set aside. In same pan melt butter until sizzling; add broccoli and garlic. Cook over medium heat, stirring occasionally, until broccoli is crisply tender (4 to 5 minutes). Stir in parsley, whipping cream and pepper. Continue cooking, stirring occasionally, until heated through (4 to 5 minutes). Stir in fettuccine, 3/4 cup Parmesan cheese and ham. Continue cooking, stirring occasionally, until heated through and cheese is melted (4 to 6 minutes). Serve with additional Parmesan cheese. **YIELD:** 4 servings.

*2 cups frozen cut broccoli can be substituted for 2 cups broccoli flowerets.

Nutrition Information (1 serving): Calories 760; Protein 24g; Carbohydrate 48g; Fat 53g; Cholesterol 170mg; Sodium 960mg.

Cannelloni

Cannelloni are large pasta tubes stuffed with a meat mixture.

Preparation time: 45 minutes • Cooking time: 47 minutes • Baking time: 50 minutes

Pasta

14 uncooked dried manicotti (pasta tubes)

Tomato Sauce

1/4 cup olive or vegetable oil
2 medium (1 cup) onions, chopped
1 (28 ounce) can Italian or plum tomatoes, coarsely chopped, reserve juice
1 (6 ounce) can tomato paste
2 tablespoons chopped fresh basil leaves*
1 teaspoon sugar
1/2 teaspoon salt
1/4 teaspoon coarsely ground pepper

Filling

1 pound bulk Italian sausage
1/4 cup chopped onion
2 teaspoons finely chopped fresh garlic
2 cups chopped fresh spinach**
1/3 cup freshly grated Parmesan cheese
2 eggs
1 tablespoon chopped fresh oregano leaves***
1/4 teaspoon coarsely ground pepper

Bechamel Sauce

1/4 cup LAND O LAKES® Butter
1/4 cup all-purpose flour
1 cup milk
1 cup whipping cream
1/4 teaspoon white pepper

1/4 cup freshly grated Parmesan cheese

Cook manicotti according to package directions. Rinse with hot water; drain. Set aside. Meanwhile, in Dutch oven heat oil; add 2 onions. Cook over medium heat, stirring constantly, until onions are soft (5 to 8 minutes). Add tomatoes, reserved juice and all remaining tomato sauce ingredients. Continue cooking, stirring occasionally, until sauce just comes to a boil (2 to 4 minutes). Reduce heat to low. Cover; continue cooking, stirring occasionally, 35 minutes. Meanwhile, in 10-inch skillet add sausage, 1/4 cup onion and garlic. Cook over medium heat, stirring constantly, until sausage is browned (10 to 12 minutes); drain off fat. Add spinach. Continue cooking, stirring occasionally, until spinach is soft (2 to 3 minutes). Place sausage mixture in large bowl. Cool 10 minutes. Stir in 1/3 cup Parmesan cheese, eggs, oregano and 1/4 teaspoon pepper. Set aside.

To prepare bechamel sauce, in 2-quart saucepan melt butter over medium heat; stir in flour until smooth and bubbly (1 minute). Add milk, whipping cream and white pepper; continue cooking, stirring occasionally, until sauce thickens (5 to 8 minutes). Heat oven to 375°. Divide filling among manicotti tubes using a small spoon to fill each tube with about 2 tablespoons filling. Place 1/4 cup tomato sauce on bottom of 13x9-inch baking pan. Place filled tubes on top of tomato sauce. Pour bechamel sauce over tubes. Top with remaining tomato sauce; sprinkle with 1/4 cup Parmesan cheese. Bake for 45 to 50 minutes or until bubbly and cheese is melted. **YIELD:** 8 servings.

*2 teaspoons dried basil leaves can be substituted for 2 tablespoons chopped fresh basil leaves.

** 1 (10 ounce) package chopped frozen spinach, thawed, drained, can be substituted for 2 cups chopped fresh spinach.

***1 teaspoon dried oregano leaves can be substituted for 1 tablespoon chopped fresh oregano leaves.

Nutrition Information (1 serving): Calories 540; Protein 18g; Carbohydrate 40g; Fat 35g; Cholesterol 140mg; Sodium 1090mg.

Angel Hair Spaghetti With Vegetables & Ham

A wonderful combination of pasta, vegetables and ham in a light, flavorful sauce.

Preparation time: 20 minutes • Cooking time: 7 minutes (pictured)

8 ounces uncooked dried angel hair pasta (very thin spaghetti)
1 (16 ounce) package frozen broccoli, carrot and cauliflower combination
2 tablespoons LAND O LAKES® Butter
1 teaspoon finely chopped fresh garlic
2 tablespoons all-purpose flour
1 1/4 cups milk
1 (8 ounce) carton (1 cup) LAND O LAKES® Light Sour Cream or dairy sour cream
1 teaspoon instant chicken bouillon granules
1/2 teaspoon dry mustard
1/2 teaspoon dried basil leaves
8 ounces cooked ham, cut into julienne strips

Freshly grated Parmesan cheese

Cook pasta according to package directions. Rinse with hot water; drain. Meanwhile, cook frozen vegetables according to package directions; drain. Meanwhile, in 2-quart saucepan melt butter until sizzling; add garlic. Cook over medium low heat, stirring constantly, until garlic is tender (30 to 60 seconds). Stir in flour until smooth and bubbly (1 minute). Add all remaining ingredients except pasta, vegetables, ham and Parmesan cheese. Cook, stirring occasionally, until sauce is thickened (4 to 6 minutes). Remove from heat; stir in vegetables and ham. Serve over hot cooked pasta; sprinkle with Parmesan cheese. **YIELD:** 8 servings.

Nutrition Information (1 serving): Calories 250; Protein 13g; Carbohydrate 31g; Fat 8g; Cholesterol 30mg; Sodium 480mg.

Skillet Pizza Casserole

Your family will love this skillet dinner with all-time favorite pizza flavors.

Preparation time: 20 minutes • Cooking time: 25 minutes (pictured)

4 ounces (2 cups) uncooked dried egg noodles
1/2 pound bulk mild Italian sausage
1/4 cup chopped green pepper
1 medium (1/2 cup) onion, chopped
1/2 cup coarsely chopped pepperoni
1/4 cup sliced 1/4-inch ripe olives
1 (15 ounce) can pizza sauce
1 cup (4 ounces) LAND O LAKES® Shredded Mozzarella Cheese

Cook noodles according to package directions. Rinse with hot water; drain. Set aside. Meanwhile, in 10-inch skillet combine sausage, green pepper and onion. Cook over medium high heat, stirring occasionally, until sausage is browned (8 to 10 minutes). Drain off fat. Stir in noodles and all remaining ingredients except cheese. Continue cooking, stirring occasionally, until mixture is heated through (10 to 15 minutes). Sprinkle with cheese. Cover; let stand 3 minutes or until cheese is melted. **YIELD:** 4 servings.

TIP: To do ahead, prepare as directed above; place in greased 1 1/2-quart casserole. Cover; refrigerate. Bake at 350° for 40 to 45 minutes or until heated through. Sprinkle with cheese. Cover; let stand 3 minutes or until cheese is melted.

Nutrition Information (1 serving): Calories 420; Protein 21g; Carbohydrate 28g; Fat 24g; Cholesterol 70mg; Sodium 1440mg.

Beef Fajitas With Fusilli Pasta

The flavors of fajitas come alive in this main dish pasta.

Preparation time: 45 minutes • Marinating time: 4 hours • Cooking time: 3 minutes • Grilling time: 12 minutes

Marinade

1/2 cup lime juice
1/2 cup olive or vegetable oil
1 medium (1/2 cup) onion, chopped
1 1/2 teaspoons cumin
1/4 teaspoon coarsely ground pepper
1 tablespoon finely chopped seeded jalapeno pepper
1 tablespoon chopped fresh cilantro or parsley
1 teaspoon finely chopped fresh garlic
1 teaspoon grated lime peel

Fajitas

1 pound (1/2 to 3/4-inch thick) beef flank steak

8 ounces (2 cups) uncooked dried fusilli (thin corkscrew or pasta twists)
1 tablespoon olive or vegetable oil
1 large onion, sliced 1/8-inch
1 large red pepper, cut in half lengthwise
1 large yellow pepper, cut in half lengthwise
1/4 cup chopped fresh cilantro or parsley

In large plastic food bag place all marinade ingredients; add steak. Tightly seal bag. Turn bag several times to coat steak well. Place in 13x9-inch pan. Refrigerate 4 hours or overnight. Prepare grill; heat until coals are ash white. Meanwhile, cook fusilli according to package directions. Rinse with hot water; drain. Toss pasta with 1 tablespoon oil; set aside. Remove steak from marinade; reserve marinade. In 1-quart saucepan cook marinade over medium heat until mixture comes to a full boil (2 to 3 minutes). Place steak on grill. Arrange onion slices and pepper halves around steak being careful not to drop any onto coals. Grill, basting occasionally with marinade, 6 minutes. Turn over steak, onion slices and pepper halves. Continue grilling for 4 to 6 minutes or until desired doneness. Slice steak across grain into 1/8-inch thick strips. Slice peppers into 1/8-inch wide strips. In large bowl combine fusilli, reserved heated marinade, steak strips, pepper strips, onion slices and cilantro. Serve with salsa, sour cream and guacamole if desired. **YIELD:** 6 servings.

Nutrition Information (1 serving): Calories 480; Protein 22g; Carbohydrate 36g; Fat 29g; Cholesterol 40mg; Sodium 45mg.

Fiesta Taco Bake

The zesty flavors of Southwestern cooking in a one-dish meal.

Preparation time: 20 minutes • Cooking time: 7 minutes • Baking time: 30 minutes

- 8 ounces (2 cups) uncooked dried radiatore (pasta nuggets)*
- 1 pound ground beef
- 1 medium (1/2 cup) onion, chopped
- 1 cup frozen whole kernel corn
- 1/2 cup mild taco sauce
- 1 (8 ounce) can tomato sauce
- 1 (4 ounce) can chopped green chilies, drained
- 1/4 teaspoon cumin
- 1/4 teaspoon salt
- 1 cup (4 ounces) LAND O LAKES® Shredded Cheddar Cheese
- 1/2 cup (2 ounces) LAND O LAKES® Shredded Mozzarella Cheese

Tomato wedges, if desired
Avocado slices, if desired

Heat oven to 350°. Cook radiatore according to package directions. Rinse with hot water; drain. Set aside. Meanwhile, in 10-inch skillet cook ground beef and onion, stirring occasionally, until browned (5 to 7 minutes); drain off fat. Stir in corn, taco sauce, tomato sauce, chilies, cumin and salt. Stir in radiatore. Spoon into greased 2-quart casserole. Sprinkle cheeses over mixture in alternating rows to form 3 Cheddar and 2 Mozzarella stripes. Bake for 25 to 30 minutes or until heated through. Garnish with tomato wedges and avocado slices. **YIELD:** 6 servings.

*6 ounces (2 cups) uncooked dried medium shell macaroni can be substituted for 8 ounces (2 cups) uncooked dried radiatore.

Nutrition Information (1 serving): Calories 440; Protein 26g; Carbohydrate 42g; Fat 19g; Cholesterol 70mg; Sodium 680mg.

Chicken & Peppers With Pasta

The fresh taste of tarragon gives this pasta toss a delicious savory flavor.

Preparation time: 30 minutes • Cooking time: 17 minutes (pictured)

6 tablespoons LAND O LAKES® Butter
1 medium onion, cut into thin wedges
1 medium red pepper, cut into strips
1 medium yellow pepper, cut into strips
1 teaspoon finely chopped fresh garlic
3 (12 ounces each) whole boneless chicken breasts, halved, skinned, cut into 3x1/2-inch strips
1 tablespoon finely chopped fresh tarragon leaves*
3/4 teaspoon salt
1/4 teaspoon coarsely ground pepper
8 ounces uncooked dried vermicelli
1 cup (4 ounces) LAND O LAKES® Shredded Mozzarella Cheese
1/2 cup freshly grated Parmesan cheese
3/4 cup half-and-half

In 12-inch skillet melt butter until sizzling; stir in onion, peppers and garlic. Cook over medium high heat until peppers are crisply tender (2 to 3 minutes). Remove vegetables from skillet with slotted spoon; set aside, reserving juices in pan. Add chicken, tarragon, salt and pepper to juices in pan. Continue cooking, stirring occasionally, until chicken is lightly browned and fork tender (7 to 9 minutes). Meanwhile, cook vermicelli according to package directions. Rinse with hot water; drain. Add vegetables, Mozzarella cheese, Parmesan cheese and half-and-half to chicken mixture. Reduce heat to medium; continue cooking until cheese is melted (3 to 5 minutes). Add hot cooked vermicelli; toss gently to coat. **YIELD:** 6 servings.

*1 teaspoon dried tarragon leaves can be substituted for 1 tablespoon fresh tarragon leaves.

Nutrition Information (1 serving): Calories 470; Protein 31g; Carbohydrate 33g; Fat 23g; Cholesterol 110mg; Sodium 690mg.

Chicken & Vegetables Over Fettuccine

Serve with crusty French bread.

Preparation time: 20 minutes • Cooking time: 22 minutes (pictured)

6 ounces uncooked dried fettuccine
1/4 cup LAND O LAKES® Butter
2 (12 ounces each) whole boneless chicken breasts, skinned, cut into 1/2-inch lengthwise strips
2 teaspoons finely chopped fresh garlic
2 cups (8 ounces) fresh mushrooms, cut into quarters
1 large onion, cut into rings
1 small green pepper, cut into strips
1 small red pepper, cut into strips
1 tablespoon all-purpose flour
1 cup whipping cream
1/4 cup dry white wine <u>or</u> chicken broth
1/2 teaspoon salt

Coarsely ground pepper
Freshly grated Parmesan cheese

Cook fettuccine according to package directions. Rinse with hot water; drain. Return to saucepan; set aside. Meanwhile, in 10-inch skillet melt butter until sizzling; add chicken and garlic. Cook over medium high heat, stirring constantly, 4 minutes. Stir in mushrooms, onion and pepper strips. Continue cooking, stirring constantly, until chicken is fork tender and vegetables are crisply tender (3 1/2 to 4 minutes). Using slotted spoon, remove chicken and vegetables; keep warm. In same skillet melt butter over medium heat; stir in flour until smooth and bubbly (1 minute). Add whipping cream, wine and salt; continue cooking, whisking constantly, until mixture comes to a full boil (6 to 8 minutes). Boil 1 minute. Add chicken and vegetables to cream mixture. Continue cooking, stirring constantly, until heated through (1 to 2 minutes). Pour mixture over hot cooked fettuccine; toss well to combine. Serve with pepper and Parmesan cheese. **YIELD:** 6 servings.

Nutrition Information (1 serving): Calories 440; Protein 24g; Carbohydrate 29g; Fat 25g; Cholesterol 120mg; Sodium 320mg.

Creamy Mushroom & Noodle Casserole

A rich, creamy sauce bakes right in the casserole for an easy one-dish meal.

Preparation time: 40 minutes • Baking time: 55 minutes

Casserole

4 ounces (2 cups) uncooked dried egg noodles
2 1/2 cups cubed 1-inch cooked chicken
2 cups frozen peas
1/4 cup LAND O LAKES® Butter, melted
1 (12 ounce) package fresh mushrooms, cut into thirds
1 medium (1/2 cup) onion, chopped
2 tablespoons all-purpose flour
1/2 teaspoon salt
1/4 teaspoon pepper
1/8 teaspoon nutmeg
2 cups half-and-half

Topping

2 cups fresh bread crumbs
1/2 cup chopped fresh parsley
2 tablespoons LAND O LAKES® Butter, melted

Cook noodles according to package directions. Rinse with hot water; drain. Heat oven to 350°. In large bowl stir together cooked noodles and all casserole ingredients except half-and-half. Stir in half-and-half. Spoon into 13x9-inch baking pan. Bake, stirring occasionally, for 30 to 35 minutes or until hot and slightly thickened. In small bowl stir together all topping ingredients. Sprinkle over hot chicken mixture. Continue baking for 15 to 20 minutes or until topping is golden brown. Let stand 5 minutes. **YIELD:** 6 servings.

Nutrition Information (1 serving): Calories 510; Protein 28g; Carbohydrate 39g; Fat 27g; Cholesterol 140mg; Sodium 520mg.

Italian Pasta & Spinach Casserole

A hearty spaghetti dish that's sure to satisfy a hungry crowd.

Preparation time: 20 minutes • Baking time: 40 minutes

8 ounces uncooked dried spaghetti
2 cups (8 ounces) LAND O LAKES® Shredded Mozzarella Cheese
1 1/2 cups LAND O LAKES® Light Sour Cream or dairy sour cream
1 (10 ounce) package frozen chopped spinach, thawed, drained
1 egg
1 teaspoon garlic salt
2 cups spaghetti sauce

Heat oven to 350°. Cook spaghetti according to package directions. Rinse with hot water; drain. Meanwhile, in large bowl stir together all remaining ingredients except spaghetti sauce; stir in hot cooked spaghetti. Place spaghetti mixture in 13x9-inch baking pan; pour spaghetti sauce over entire surface. Bake for 30 to 40 minutes or until heated through. **YIELD:** 12 servings.

Nutrition Information (1 serving): Calories 215; Protein 11g; Carbohydrate 26g; Fat 8g; Cholesterol 34mg; Sodium 520mg.

Curried Chicken & Vegetables

The flavors of India are reflected in this pasta made with a blend of spices.

Preparation time: 30 minutes • Cooking time: 34 minutes (pictured)

- 6 ounces (1 cup) uncooked dried rosamarina pasta (orzo)
- 3 tablespoons LAND O LAKES® Butter
- 2 medium (1 cup) onions, chopped
- 2 teaspoons grated fresh gingerroot
- 1 tablespoon curry powder
- 1 teaspoon coriander
- 1 teaspoon cumin
- 1 teaspoon turmeric
- 1/4 teaspoon cardamom
- 1 pound whole boneless chicken breasts, skinned, cut into 1-inch pieces
- 1 cup cauliflower flowerets
- 2 medium (1 cup) carrots, sliced 1/8-inch
- 1 (10 1/4 ounce) can chicken broth
- 1/2 cup frozen baby peas
- 1 tablespoon lime juice

Condiments

- Major Grey chutney
- Coarsely chopped peanuts or cashews
- Raisins
- Shredded coconut
- Sliced bananas

Prepare pasta according to package directions. Rinse with hot water; drain. Set aside. Meanwhile, in 10-inch skillet melt butter until sizzling; add onions and gingerroot. Cook over medium heat, stirring occasionally, until onions are soft (5 to 8 minutes). Add curry, coriander, cumin, turmeric and cardamom. Continue cooking, stirring constantly, 30 seconds. Add chicken. Continue cooking, stirring constantly, until chicken is lightly browned (6 to 8 minutes). Add cauliflower, carrots and chicken broth. Cover; reduce heat to medium low. Continue cooking, stirring occasionally, until carrots and cauliflower are crisply tender (10 to 12 minutes). Stir in pasta, peas and lime juice. Continue cooking, stirring occasionally, until heated through (3 to 5 minutes). Serve with condiments. **YIELD:** 4 servings.

Nutrition Information (1 serving): Calories 430; Protein 34g; Carbohydrate 43g; Fat 13g; Cholesterol 90mg; Sodium 420mg.

Rigatoni & Spicy Sausage With Paprika Sauce

Italian sausage melds with a creamy sauce to flavor rigatoni.

Preparation time: 20 minutes • Cooking time: 38 minutes

8 ounces (3 cups) uncooked dried rigatoni
1 tablespoon olive or vegetable oil
1 tablespoon finely chopped fresh garlic
1 pound Italian sausage links
2 tablespoons water
1 1/2 cups whipping cream
4 teaspoons paprika
1/4 teaspoon ground red pepper
1/2 cup 1-inch pieces green pepper
1/4 cup 1/4-inch sliced ripe olives
1/4 cup freshly grated Parmesan cheese
2 medium (2 cups) ripe tomatoes, peeled, seeded, cut into 1-inch pieces
2 tablespoons chopped fresh basil leaves*
2 tablespoons chopped fresh oregano leaves**

Freshly grated Parmesan cheese, if desired

In Dutch oven heat oil; add garlic. Cook over medium heat, stirring constantly, until garlic is tender (30 to 60 seconds). Add sausage links and water. Cover; cook, turning links once, 10 minutes. Uncover; continue cooking, adding additional water if needed, until fully cooked (12 to 15 minutes). Remove links; drain on paper towels. When cool, cut into 1/2-inch diagonal pieces; set aside. Drain off fat and water. In same pan, with wire whisk, stir together whipping cream, paprika and ground red pepper. Cook over medium heat, stirring occasionally, until mixture just comes to a boil (3 to 4 minutes). Stir in cut sausage, green peppers, olives, 1/4 cup Parmesan cheese, tomato, basil and oregano. Continue cooking, stirring occasionally, until heated through (6 to 8 minutes). Meanwhile, cook rigatoni according to package directions. Rinse with hot water; drain. Serve sausage mixture over hot rigatoni. Sprinkle with additional Parmesan cheese. **YIELD:** 6 servings.

*2 teaspoons dried basil leaves can be substituted for 2 tablespoons chopped fresh basil leaves.

**2 teaspoons dried oregano leaves can be substituted for 2 tablespoons chopped fresh oregano leaves.

Nutrition Information (1 serving): Calories 520; Protein 16g; Carbohydrate 35g; Fat 36g; Cholesterol 110mg; Sodium 480mg.

Sausage & Vegetable Pasta Supper

Smoked sausage, vegetables and pasta are combined in a skillet meal tossed with cheese.

Preparation time: 20 minutes • Cooking time: 15 minutes

8 ounces (3 cups) uncooked dried rigatoni*
2 tablespoons LAND O LAKES® Butter
1 pound cooked smoked sausage, cut into 1/2-inch slices
1 green pepper, cut into 1-inch pieces
1 medium onion, cut into 1/2-inch slices
1/2 teaspoon finely chopped fresh garlic
1 (28 ounce) can whole tomatoes, drained, cut up
2 cups (8 ounces) LAND O LAKES® Shredded Monterey Jack Cheese

Cook rigatoni according to package directions. Rinse with hot water; drain. Set aside. Meanwhile, in Dutch oven melt butter until sizzling; add sausage, green pepper, onion and garlic. Cook over medium heat, stirring occasionally, until green pepper is crisply tender (8 to 10 minutes). Stir in rigatoni, tomatoes and cheese. Continue cooking, stirring occasionally, until heated through (3 to 5 minutes). **YIELD:** 6 servings.

* 8 ounces (2 1/2 cups) uncooked dried rotini (corkscrew or pasta twists) can be substituted for 8 ounces (3 cups) uncooked dried rigatoni.

Nutrition Information (1 serving): Calories 600; Protein 26g; Carbohydrate 37g; Fat 39g; Cholesterol 100mg; Sodium 970mg.

Angel Hair Pasta With Basil & Shrimp

Basil accents shrimp and tomatoes served over pasta.

Preparation time: 20 minutes • Cooking time: 16 minutes (pictured)

8 ounces uncooked dried angel hair pasta (very thin spaghetti) or vermicelli
1/4 cup olive or vegetable oil
1 teaspoon finely chopped fresh garlic
1 pound (40 to 45 medium) fresh or frozen raw shrimp, shelled, deveined, rinsed
1/4 cup chopped fresh parsley
1/2 cup dry white wine or chicken broth
2 (28 ounce) cans Italian or plum tomatoes, drained, cut up
3 tablespoons chopped fresh basil leaves*

Freshly grated Parmesan cheese

Cook pasta according to package directions. Rinse with hot water; drain. Toss with 1 tablespoon oil. Keep warm. In 10-inch skillet heat remaining oil; add garlic. Cook over medium high heat, stirring constantly, until garlic is tender (30 to 60 seconds). Add shrimp; continue cooking, stirring constantly, until shrimp turn pink (1 to 2 minutes). Remove shrimp; set aside. Stir in all remaining ingredients except Parmesan cheese. Continue cooking, stirring occasionally, until liquid is reduced by half (7 to 10 minutes). Add shrimp; continue cooking until shrimp are heated through (2 to 3 minutes). Serve over hot cooked pasta; sprinkle with Parmesan cheese. **YIELD:** 6 servings.

*2 teaspoons dried basil leaves can be substituted for 3 tablespoons chopped fresh basil leaves.

Nutrition Information (1 serving): Calories 300; Protein 10g; Carbohydrate 41g; Fat 10g; Cholesterol 28mg; Sodium 490mg.

Sauteed Scallops With Yellow Tomato Sauce

If yellow tomatoes are unavailable, use ripe red tomatoes instead.

Preparation time: 15 minutes • Cooking time: 24 minutes

8 ounces uncooked dried vermicelli
1 tablespoon olive or vegetable oil
1/2 teaspoon finely chopped fresh garlic
1 1/2 pounds fresh or frozen bay scallops
1/2 cup dry white wine or chicken broth
1 (10 1/4 ounce) can chicken broth
1 medium (1 tablespoon) shallot, finely chopped *
3 medium (3 cups) ripe yellow or red tomatoes peeled, seeded, cut into 1-inch pieces
2 tablespoons LAND O LAKES® Butter
1 tablespoon chopped fresh herbs (thyme, rosemary, basil, etc.)**
1/4 teaspoon pepper

Cook vermicelli according to package directions. Rinse with hot water; drain. Meanwhile, in 10-inch skillet heat oil; add garlic. Cook over medium heat, stirring constantly, until garlic is tender (30 to 60 seconds). Add scallops; continue cooking, stirring constantly, until scallops just turn opaque (2 to 4 minutes). Drain scallops reserving 1/4 cup liquid; set aside. In same skillet add reserved 1/4 cup scallop liquid, wine, chicken broth and shallot. Cook over medium heat, stirring occasionally, until liquid is reduced by half (12 to 14 minutes). Stir in tomatoes; continue cooking, stirring occasionally, until heated through (2 to 3 minutes). Stir in scallops, butter, herbs and pepper; continue cooking until heated through (1 to 2 minutes). Serve over hot cooked vermicelli. **YIELD:** 6 servings.

* 1 tablespoon chopped onion can be substituted for 1 medium (1 tablespoon) shallot, finely chopped.

** 1 teaspoon dried herbs (thyme, rosemary, basil, etc.) can be substituted for 1 tablespoon chopped fresh herbs.

Nutrition Information (1 serving): Calories 330; Protein 25g; Carbohydrate 35g; Fat 8g; Cholesterol 50mg; Sodium 390mg.

Italian Shrimp Pasta Toss

Shrimp, fettuccine and fresh vegetables are topped with Mozzarella cheese.

Preparation time: 30 minutes • Cooking time: 11 minutes

8 ounces uncooked dried fettuccine
1/4 cup LAND O LAKES® Butter
1 cup broccoli flowerets
1 cup (4 ounces) sliced fresh mushrooms
2 medium (1 cup) carrots, sliced 1/4-inch
1 medium (1/2 cup) onion, chopped
12 ounces fresh or frozen medium raw shrimp, shelled, deveined, rinsed
1/2 teaspoon finely chopped fresh garlic
1 teaspoon dried basil leaves
1/2 teaspoon salt
1/4 teaspoon coarsely ground pepper
1 1/2 cups (6 ounces) LAND O LAKES® Shredded Mozzarella Cheese

Cook fettuccine according to package directions. Rinse with hot water; drain. Meanwhile, in 10-inch skillet melt butter until sizzling; add broccoli, mushrooms, carrots, onion, shrimp and garlic. Cook over medium heat, stirring occasionally, until vegetables are crisply tender and shrimp turn pink (5 to 7 minutes). Stir in basil, salt and pepper. Add fettuccine and cheese. Continue cooking, tossing gently, until cheese is melted (2 to 4 minutes). **YIELD:** 6 servings.

VARIATION

Italian Pasta Toss: Omit shrimp.

Nutrition Information (1 serving): Calories 370; Protein 25g; Carbohydrate 33g; Fat 14g; Cholesterol 120mg; Sodium 500mg.

Shrimp & Artichoke Kabobs

Shrimp and marinated artichoke kabobs are served over a lemon-zested pasta.

Preparation time: 40 minutes • Grilling time: 10 minutes (pictured)

9 ounces uncooked fresh linguini*
1 pound (about 24 medium) fresh or frozen raw shrimp
1 medium red onion, cut into 12 wedges
2 (6 ounce) jars marinated artichokes, reserve marinade

6 (12-inch) metal skewers

Basting Sauce
2 teaspoons dried basil leaves
1/2 teaspoon salt
1/2 teaspoon coarsely ground pepper
Dash ground red pepper
1/2 teaspoon finely chopped fresh garlic
2 tablespoons olive or vegetable oil

2 teaspoons grated lemon peel

Prepare grill; heat until coals are ash white. Cook linguini according to package directions. Rinse with hot water; drain. Place in large bowl; set aside. Meanwhile, peel and devein shrimp, leaving tail intact. (If shrimp are frozen, do not thaw; peel under running cold water.) Alternate shrimp, onion and artichokes on skewers. In small bowl stir together 2 tablespoons reserved marinade and all basting sauce ingredients except lemon peel; brush over kabobs. Place kabobs on grill. Grill, basting and turning occasionally, for 7 to 10 minutes or until shrimp turn pink. Meanwhile, add remaining artichoke marinade and lemon peel to linguini; toss to coat. Serve kabobs with hot cooked linguini. **YIELD:** 6 servings.

* 9 ounces uncooked dried linguini can be substituted for 9 ounces uncooked fresh linguini.

Nutrition Information (1 serving): Calories 300; Protein 18g; Carbohydrate 40g; Fat 8g; Cholesterol 85mg; Sodium 240mg.

Seafood Lasagna

Noodles and seafood are layered with a rich, creamy sauce.

Preparation time: 45 minutes • Cooking time: 7 minutes • Baking time: 45 minutes

9 uncooked dried lasagna noodles

Sauce

3 tablespoons LAND O LAKES® Butter
1/4 cup all-purpose flour
2 teaspoons finely chopped fresh garlic
1 1/2 cups milk
1/2 cup dry white wine <u>or</u> milk
1 teaspoon nutmeg
1/2 teaspoon salt
1/4 teaspoon pepper
1/8 teaspoon hot pepper sauce

Ricotta Filling

2 eggs
3/4 cup freshly grated Parmesan cheese
1/2 cup chopped fresh parsley
1 (15 ounce) carton (2 cups) ricotta cheese
1 (4 ounce) jar sliced pimiento, drained

Layers

1 (12 ounce) package small frozen cooked shrimp, thawed, drained, <u>reserve 12 for garnish</u>
1 (8 ounce) package frozen salad chunks imitation sea stixs, thawed, drained
3 cups (12 ounces) LAND O LAKES® Shredded Swiss Cheese

12 fresh parsley sprigs

Heat oven to 375°. Cook noodles according to package directions. Rinse with hot water; drain. Set aside. In 2-quart saucepan melt butter until sizzling; stir in flour and garlic until smooth and bubbly (1 minute). Add 1 1/2 cups milk; continue cooking over medium heat, stirring occasionally, until mixture comes to a full boil (4 to 5 minutes); boil 1 minute. Stir in all remaining sauce ingredients; set aside. In small bowl slightly beat eggs; stir in all remaining ricotta filling ingredients. In greased 13x9-inch baking pan layer <u>1/3</u> noodles, <u>1/2</u> ricotta filling, <u>1/2</u> shrimp, <u>1/2</u> sea stixs, <u>1/3</u> sauce and <u>1/3</u> Swiss cheese. Repeat layering. Top with remaining noodles, sauce and Swiss cheese. Cover with aluminum foil; bake 25 minutes. Uncover; continue baking for 15 to 20 minutes or until lightly brown around edges. Let stand 10 minutes. Garnish each serving with reserved shrimp and parsley sprigs. **YIELD**: 12 servings.

TIP: 8 ounces crabmeat can be substituted for 8 ounces imitation sea stixs.

Nutrition Information (1 serving): Calories 370; Protein 28g; Carbohydrate 20g; Fat 18g; Cholesterol 150mg; Sodium 480mg.

Lasagna Roll-ups With Cream Sauce

These lasagna roll-ups are filled with the fresh tastes of garden vegetables and herbs.

Preparation time: 45 minutes • Cooking time: 13 minutes • Baking time: 30 minutes

Lasagna

8 uncooked dried lasagna noodles

2 tablespoons LAND O LAKES® Butter
1 teaspoon finely chopped fresh garlic
1/2 cup coarsely chopped red onion
1 medium (1 cup) zucchini, sliced 1/8-inch
1 medium (1 cup) yellow, red <u>or</u> green pepper, cut into 1-inch pieces
1/2 teaspoon salt
1/4 teaspoon pepper
2 tablespoons chopped fresh basil leaves*
1 teaspoon chopped fresh oregano leaves**
1 egg, slightly beaten
1 cup (4 ounces) LAND O LAKES® Shredded Mozzarella Cheese
1/2 cup freshly grated Parmesan cheese
1 (15 ounce) carton ricotta cheese***
2 medium (2 cups) ripe tomatoes, cut into 1/2-inch pieces

Herb Sauce

2 tablespoons LAND O LAKES® Butter
2 tablespoons all-purpose flour
1/4 teaspoon salt
1/4 teaspoon pepper
1 cup milk
1 cup (4 ounces) LAND O LAKES® Shredded Mozzarella Cheese
1/4 cup chopped fresh parsley
1 tablespoon chopped fresh basil leaves****
2 tablespoons freshly grated Parmesan cheese

Heat oven to 350°. Cook lasagna noodles according to package directions. Rinse with hot water; drain. Meanwhile, in 10-inch skillet melt 2 tablespoons butter until sizzling; stir in garlic. Add all remaining lasagna ingredients <u>except</u> egg, 1 cup Mozzarella cheese, 1/2 cup Parmesan cheese, ricotta cheese and tomatoes. Cook over medium heat, stirring occasionally, until vegetables are crisply tender (5 to 6 minutes). Meanwhile, in large bowl stir together egg and cheeses. Stir in tomatoes and cooked vegetables. Place about 1/2 cup filling on one end of each lasagna noodle. Roll up lasagna noodle jelly roll fashion. (Some filling will spill out each end.) Place, seam side down, in 12x8-inch baking pan. Fill in around roll-ups with excess filling; set aside.

In 2-quart saucepan melt 2 tablespoons butter over medium heat; stir in flour, 1/4 teaspoon salt and 1/4 teaspoon pepper until smooth and bubbly (1 minute). Add milk; continue cooking, stirring occasionally, until sauce begins to thicken (1 to 2 minutes). Stir in 1 cup Mozzarella cheese, parsley and 1 tablespoon basil. Continue cooking, stirring occasionally, until cheese is melted (2 to 4 minutes). Pour over lasagna roll-ups; sprinkle with 2 tablespoons Parmesan cheese. Bake for 25 to 30 minutes or until heated through. **YIELD:** 8 servings.

*2 teaspoons dried basil leaves can be substituted for 2 tablespoons chopped fresh basil leaves.

**1/4 teaspoon dried oregano leaves can be substituted for 1 teaspoon chopped fresh oregano leaves.

***1 (12 ounce) carton cottage cheese can be substituted for 1 (15 ounce) carton ricotta cheese.

****1 teaspoon dried basil leaves can be substituted for 1 tablespoon chopped fresh basil leaves.

Nutrition Information (1 serving): Calories 360; Protein 22g; Carbohydrate 27g; Fat 19g; Cholesterol 80mg; Sodium 650mg.

Roasted Red Pepper & Scallop Fettuccine

Roasted red pepper sauce adds color and flavor to scallops served over pasta.

Preparation time: 30 minutes • Baking time: 35 minutes • Cooking time: 14 minutes (pictured)

2 whole red peppers
16 ounces uncooked dried fettuccine
1/4 cup LAND O LAKES® Butter
2 teaspoons finely chopped fresh garlic
1/2 cup sliced green onions
1 1/2 pounds fresh or frozen large scallops
1 (16 ounce) carton (2 cups) LAND O LAKES® Light Sour Cream or dairy sour cream

Salt
Coarsely ground pepper

Heat oven to 400°. Place whole red peppers on cookie sheet. Bake, turning occasionally, for 25 to 35 minutes or until skins are blackened. Cool; remove skins and seeds. In 5-cup blender container puree peppers on High until smooth (30 to 45 seconds). Set aside. Cook fettuccine according to package directions. Rinse with hot water; drain. Meanwhile, in 10-inch skillet melt butter until sizzling; add garlic. Cook over medium heat, stirring occasionally, 1 minute. Add green onions and scallops. Continue cooking, stirring occasionally, until scallops are tender (5 to 7 minutes). Stir in Light Sour Cream and red pepper puree until well mixed. Continue cooking until heated through (4 to 6 minutes). In large bowl toss together scallop mixture and hot fettuccine. Season to taste.
YIELD: 8 servings.

Nutrition Information (1 serving): Calories 400; Protein 24g; Carbohydrate 51g; Fat 11g; Cholesterol 55mg; Sodium 240mg.

Country Vegetable Lasagna

You won't miss the meat in this flavorful cheese lasagna.

Preparation time: 45 minutes • Cooking time: 42 minutes • Baking time: 35 minutes (pictured)

Pasta

9 uncooked dried lasagna noodles

Sauce

3 tablespoons olive or vegetable oil
2 cups (8 ounces) coarsely chopped fresh mushrooms
1 medium (1 cup) green pepper, chopped
1 medium (1/2 cup) onion, chopped
1 teaspoon finely chopped fresh garlic
1/4 cup chopped fresh parsley
1 (28 ounce) can whole tomatoes, undrained, cut up
1 (12 ounce) can tomato paste
2 teaspoons sugar
1 teaspoon dried basil leaves
1 teaspoon dried oregano leaves
2 bay leaves

Cheese Mixture

1/4 cup freshly grated Parmesan cheese
1 (15 ounce) carton ricotta cheese*
2 eggs
1/4 teaspoon pepper

3 cups (12 ounces) LAND O LAKES® Shredded Mozzarella Cheese
1/4 cup freshly grated Parmesan cheese

Cook lasagna noodles according to package directions. Rinse with hot water; drain. Meanwhile, in 10-inch skillet heat oil; add mushrooms, green pepper, onion and garlic. Cook over medium heat, stirring occasionally, until vegetables are crisply tender (7 to 9 minutes). Stir in all remaining sauce ingredients. Continue cooking, stirring occasionally, until mixture comes to a full boil (2 to 3 minutes). Reduce heat to low; continue cooking, stirring occasionally, 30 minutes. Remove bay leaves. Meanwhile, in medium bowl stir together 1/4 cup Parmesan cheese, ricotta cheese, eggs and pepper. Heat oven to 350°. On bottom of 13x9-inch baking pan spread 1 cup sauce. Top with 3 lasagna noodles, 1/3 cheese mixture, 1/3 sauce and 1 cup Mozzarella cheese. Repeat layers 2 more times, ending with Mozzarella cheese. Sprinkle with 1/4 cup Parmesan cheese. Bake for 30 to 35 minutes or until bubbly and heated through. Let stand 10 minutes. **YIELD:** 8 servings.

*2 cups cottage cheese can be substituted for 1 (15 ounce) carton ricotta cheese.

Nutrition Information (1 serving): Calories 460; Protein 29g; Carbohydrate 40g; Fat 21g; Cholesterol 110mg; Sodium 1010mg.

Country Pasta With Mozzarella

A hearty, home-style pasta filled with bacon, broccoli and Mozzarella cheese.

Preparation time: 15 minutes • Cooking time: 18 minutes (pictured)

8 ounces uncooked rigatoni
8 slices bacon, cut into 1-inch pieces
2 cups broccoli flowerets
1/2 teaspoon finely chopped fresh garlic
2 cups (8 ounces) LAND O LAKES® Shredded Mozzarella Cheese
1/4 cup grated Parmesan cheese
1/8 teaspoon ground red pepper
1/4 cup chopped fresh parsley

Cook rigatoni according to package directions. Rinse with hot water; drain. Set aside. Meanwhile, in 10-inch skillet cook bacon over medium high heat, stirring occasionally, until bacon is crisp (6 to 8 minutes). Reduce heat to medium. Add broccoli and garlic. Cook, stirring occasionally, until broccoli is crisply tender (4 to 5 minutes). Add rigatoni, Mozzarella cheese, Parmesan cheese and ground red pepper. Continue cooking, stirring occasionally, until cheese is melted (3 to 5 minutes). Sprinkle with parsley. **YIELD:** 6 servings.

Nutrition Information (1 serving): Calories 320; Protein 20g; Carbohydrate 30g; Fat 13g; Cholesterol 30mg; Sodium 420mg.

Quick Tortellini Supper

Fresh pasta combines with mushrooms, peas and cheese for an easy meal.

Preparation time: 15 minutes • Cooking time: 10 minutes (pictured)

18 ounces (4 cups) fresh tortellini*
1/4 cup LAND O LAKES® Butter
1 cup sliced fresh mushrooms
1 (10 ounce) package frozen peas, thawed
1 1/2 cups (6 ounces) LAND O LAKES® Shredded Cheddar Cheese
Salt and pepper

Cook tortellini according to package directions. Rinse with hot water; drain. Set aside. In 10-inch skillet melt butter until sizzling; add mushrooms. Cook over medium heat, stirring occasionally, until tender (3 to 5 minutes). Stir in tortellini and peas; continue cooking until heated through (3 to 5 minutes). Stir in 1 cup cheese; salt and pepper to taste. Sprinkle with remaining cheese. **YIELD:** 4 servings.

*7 ounces (1 1/2 cups) uncooked dried tortellini or 8 ounces (2 1/2 cups) uncooked dried medium macaroni shells can be substituted for 18 ounces (4 cups) fresh tortellini. Cook according to package directions; drain.

Nutrition Information (1 serving): Calories 650; Protein 34g; Carbohydrate 47g; Fat 36g; Cholesterol 230mg; Sodium 940mg.

Pasta Primavera

A variety of colorful, flavorful vegetables simmer in a white wine sauce.

Preparation time: 30 minutes • Cooking time: 19 minutes (pictured)

1 (9 ounce) package uncooked fresh linguine*
3 tablespoons olive or vegetable oil
1 medium red onion, thinly sliced
1/2 teaspoon finely chopped fresh garlic
2 medium (2 cups) yellow summer squash, halved lengthwise, sliced 1/8-inch
1 medium (1 cup) ripe tomato, cubed 1/2-inch
1 medium red or green pepper, cut into 1/4-inch strips
1 pound (24) asparagus spears, trimmed, cut into thirds
1/2 cup dry white wine or chicken broth
2 tablespoons chopped fresh dill**
1/4 teaspoon salt
1/4 teaspoon coarsely ground pepper

1/4 cup freshly grated Parmesan cheese

Freshly grated Parmesan cheese

Cook linguine according to package directions. Rinse with hot water; drain. Meanwhile, in 10-inch skillet heat oil; add onion and garlic. Cook over medium heat, stirring occasionally, until onion is crisply tender (3 to 4 minutes). Add squash, tomato, red pepper and asparagus. Continue cooking, stirring occasionally, until vegetables are crisply tender (8 to 10 minutes). Stir in wine, dill weed, salt and pepper. Continue cooking, stirring occasionally, until heated through (4 to 5 minutes). Serve over hot cooked linguine with 1/4 cup Parmesan cheese. Serve with additional Parmesan cheese. **YIELD:** 6 servings.

* 9 ounces uncooked dried linguine can be substituted for 1 (9 ounce) package uncooked fresh linguine.

** 2 teaspoons dried dill weed can be substituted for 2 tablespoons chopped fresh dill.

Nutrition Information (1 serving): Calories 290; Protein 11g; Carbohydrates 41g; Fat 9g; Cholesterol 2mg; Sodium 180mg.

Soups

Add pasta to some traditional favorites and what do you get? A savory, new temptation that tastes even better the next day. You can either use these recipes to create a flavorful side dish or a hearty, one-dish meal.

Vegetable & Pasta Pesto Soup

Use homemade or purchased pesto to stir into this vegetable soup for extra flavor.

Preparation time: 45 minutes • Cooking time: 43 minutes (pictured on page 106)

3 tablespoons olive or vegetable oil
1/2 cup sliced 1/8-inch leeks
2 medium (1 cup) onions, chopped
5 (14 1/2 ounce) cans low sodium chicken broth
2 medium (1 cup) carrots, sliced 1/8-inch
2 stalks (1 cup) celery, sliced 1/8-inch
1 tablespoon chopped fresh thyme leaves*
1/4 pound (1 cup) fresh green beans, cut into thirds
2 cups fresh spinach, torn into bite-size pieces**
1 medium (1 cup) ripe tomato, peeled, seeded, cut into 1/2-inch pieces
1 medium (1 cup) zucchini, cut in half lengthwise, then into 1/2-inch slices
1 (15 ounce) can cannellini beans, rinsed, drained
1/2 teaspoon salt
1/4 teaspoon pepper
7 ounces (1 1/2 cups) uncooked dried pasta rings

1/2 cup pesto sauce***
Freshly grated Parmesan cheese

In Dutch oven heat oil; add leeks and onions. Cook over medium heat, stirring occasionally, until onions are soft (5 to 8 minutes). Add chicken broth, carrots, celery and thyme. Cook over high heat until soup just comes to a boil (4 to 5 minutes). Cover; reduce heat to medium. Continue cooking until carrots are crisply tender (13 to 15 minutes). Add green beans; continue cooking 4 minutes. Stir in spinach, tomato, zucchini, cannellini beans, salt and pepper. Continue cooking, stirring occasionally, 5 minutes. Add pasta. Continue cooking, stirring occasionally, until pasta is tender (5 to 6 minutes). To serve, ladle soup into bowls. Spoon 1 tablespoon pesto sauce into each bowl; sprinkle with Parmesan cheese. **YIELD:** 8 servings.

* 1 teaspoon dried thyme leaves can be substituted for 1 tablespoon chopped fresh thyme leaves.

** 1 (10 ounce) package frozen chopped spinach, thawed, can be substituted for 2 cups fresh spinach, torn into bite-size pieces.

*** Prepare Fresh Pesto Sauce on page 123 or use purchased pesto sauce.

Nutrition Information (1 serving): Calories 320; Protein 12g; Carbohydrate 35g; Fat 15g; Cholesterol 0mg; Sodium 270mg.

Easy Turkey Soup

This easy soup features orzo, a rice shaped pasta.

Preparation time: 15 minutes • Cooking time: 30 minutes

- 2 cups cubed 1/2-inch cooked turkey
- 2 cups water
- 1 stalk (1/2 cup) celery, sliced 1/4-inch
- 1 (10 ounce) package frozen mixed vegetables
- 1 (14 1/2 ounce) can chicken broth
- 1/4 teaspoon dried thyme leaves
- 1/8 teaspoon pepper
- 3 ounces (1/2 cup) uncooked dried rosamarina pasta (orzo) or pasta rings

In 4-quart saucepan combine all ingredients except pasta. Cook over high heat, stirring occasionally, until mixture comes to a full boil (10 to 15 minutes). Add pasta; reduce heat to low. Cover; continue cooking, stirring occasionally, until pasta is tender (12 to 15 minutes). **YIELD:** 6 servings.

Nutrition Information (1 serving): Calories 150; Protein 18g; Carbohydrate 12g; Fat 3g; Cholesterol 36mg; Sodium 280mg.

ABC Vegetables N' Chili

Kids will love this hearty pasta soup.

Preparation time: 10 minutes • Cooking time: 1 hour 10 minutes (pictured)

1 medium (1/2 cup) onion, chopped
1 pound lean ground beef
3 cups water
1 (15 ounce) can tomato sauce
1 (14 1/2 ounce) can stewed tomatoes, cut up
1 to 2 teaspoons chili powder
1 teaspoon salt
1/4 teaspoon pepper
2 cups frozen mixed vegetable combination
1 cup uncooked dried alphabet-shaped pasta or pasta rings

LAND O LAKES® Shredded Cheddar Cheese, if desired

In Dutch oven combine onion and ground beef. Cook over medium high heat, stirring occasionally, until beef is browned (10 to 15 minutes); drain off fat. Return beef to Dutch oven. Add water, tomato sauce, stewed tomatoes, chili powder, salt and pepper. Continue cooking, stirring occasionally, until chili just comes to a boil (10 to 15 minutes). Add vegetable combination and pasta. Continue cooking, stirring occasionally, until chili just comes to a boil (5 to 10 minutes). Reduce heat to medium low. Continue cooking, stirring often, 20 to 30 minutes or until flavors are blended. Sprinkle cheese over individual bowls of chili. **YIELD**: 8 servings.

Nutrition Information (1 serving): Calories 210; Protein 14g; Carbohydrate 23g; Fat 8g; Cholesterol 36mg; Sodium 770mg.

Broccoli Cheese Soup

Sharp Cheddar cheese flavors this broccoli and pasta soup.

Preparation time: 20 minutes • Cooking time: 22 minutes (pictured)

- 4 ounces (1 cup) uncooked dried gemelli (double twist pasta) or rotini (corkscrew or pasta twists)
- 2 cups small broccoli flowerets*
- 1/4 cup LAND O LAKES® Butter
- 1/2 cup sliced 1/8-inch leeks
- 1 medium (1 tablespoon) shallot, finely chopped**
- 3 tablespoons all-purpose flour
- 1/4 teaspoon dry mustard
- 1/4 teaspoon coarsely ground pepper
- 2 medium (1 cup) carrots, shredded
- 2 (14 1/2 ounce) cans low sodium chicken broth
- 1 teaspoon Worcestershire sauce
- 1 cup half-and-half or milk
- 1 1/2 cups (6 ounces) LAND O LAKES® Shredded Sharp Cheddar Cheese

Cook gemelli according to package directions adding broccoli during last 6 minutes of cooking time. Rinse with hot water; drain. Set aside. Meanwhile, in Dutch oven melt butter until sizzling; add leeks and shallot. Cook over medium heat, stirring occasionally, until soft (3 to 5 minutes). Stir in flour, mustard and pepper. Continue cooking 1 minute. Add carrots, chicken broth and Worcestershire sauce. Continue cooking, stirring occasionally, until soup just comes to a boil (3 to 5 minutes). Add half-and-half. Continue cooking, stirring occasionally, until heated through (2 to 4 minutes). Add cheese. Continue cooking, stirring constantly, until cheese is melted (1 to 2 minutes). Add gemelli and broccoli. Continue cooking until heated through (3 to 5 minutes).
YIELD: 6 servings.

* 1 (10 3/4 ounce) package chopped frozen broccoli, thawed, can be substituted for 2 cups small broccoli flowerets. Do not cook with gemelli. Add to soup when gemelli is added.

** 1 tablespoon chopped onion can be substituted for 1 medium (1 tablespoon) shallot, finely chopped.

Nutrition Information (1 serving): Calories 350; Protein 14g; Carbohydrate 24g; Fat 22g; Cholesterol 65mg; Sodium 330mg.

Seafood Chowder

Shrimp, clams and white fish make this chowder extra special.

Preparation time: 45 minutes • Cooking time: 30 minutes

- **1/4 cup LAND O LAKES® Butter**
- **2 medium (1 cup) onions, chopped**
- **2 medium (1 cup) carrots, shredded**
- **1 pound fresh <u>or</u> frozen raw medium shrimp, shelled, deveined, rinsed**
- **2 (6 1/2 ounce) cans chopped clams, drained, <u>reserve juice</u>**
- **4 cups water**
- **1 (8 ounce) bottle clam juice**
- **4 ounces (1 cup) uncooked dried cavatelli <u>or</u> medium pasta shells**
- **1 1/2 pounds boneless white fish fillets (cod, haddock, ocean perch, orange roughy, etc.), skinned, cut into bite-size pieces**
- **1/4 cup chopped fresh parsley**
- **2 cups (1 pint) half-and-half**
- **2 teaspoons paprika**
- **1/4 teaspoon salt**
- **1/4 teaspoon coarsely ground pepper**

In Dutch oven melt butter until sizzling; add onions and carrots. Cook over medium heat, stirring occasionally, until onions are soft (5 to 8 minutes). Add shrimp. Continue cooking, stirring constantly, until shrimp just turn pink (2 to 3 minutes). Place shrimp mixture in medium bowl; set aside. In same pan bring <u>reserved clam juice</u>, water and bottled clam juice to a full boil. Add cavatelli. Continue cooking over medium heat 10 minutes. Add fish. Continue cooking, stirring occasionally, until fish just turns opaque (2 to 3 minutes). Add reserved shrimp mixture, clams, parsley, half-and-half, paprika, salt and pepper. Continue cooking, stirring occasionally, until heated through (5 to 6 minutes). **YIELD:** 8 servings.

Nutrition Information (1 serving): Calories 350; Protein 35g; Carbohydrate 18g; Fat 15g; Cholesterol 170mg; Sodium 380mg.

Sausage N' Pasta Stew

Tomatoes, pasta, sausage and beans combine in this hearty stew.

Preparation time: 20 minutes • Cooking time: 36 minutes (pictured)

1/4 cup chopped onion
3/4 pound sliced 1/2-inch Italian sausage links
1/2 teaspoon finely chopped fresh garlic
1 cup water
2 (28 ounce) cans whole tomatoes, undrained, cut up
2 teaspoons sugar
1/2 teaspoon Italian herb seasoning*
3 ounces (1 cup) uncooked dried rotini (corkscrew or pasta twists)
2 cups frozen cut broccoli
1 (15 ounce) can Great Northern beans, rinsed, drained

Freshly grated Parmesan cheese, if desired

In Dutch oven cook onion, sausage and garlic over medium high heat until sausage is browned (8 to 10 minutes); drain off fat. Add water, tomatoes, sugar and Italian herb seasoning. Continue cooking until mixture comes to a full boil (6 to 8 minutes); stir in rotini. Reduce heat to medium. Continue cooking, stirring occasionally, until rotini is tender (8 to 11 minutes). Stir in broccoli and beans. Continue cooking, stirring occasionally, until broccoli is crisply tender (5 to 7 minutes). Serve with Parmesan cheese. **YIELD:** 6 servings.

*1/8 teaspoon each dried oregano leaves, dried marjoram leaves and dried basil leaves and 1/16 teaspoon rubbed sage can be substituted for 1/2 teaspoon Italian herb seasoning.

Nutrition Information (1 serving): Calories 230; Protein 13g; Carbohydrate 28g; Fat 8g; Cholesterol 22mg; Sodium 470mg.

Chili Spiced Beef & Bean Stew

It's neither chili nor spaghetti, but a spicy, rich stew with ground beef and pork sausage.

Preparation time: 15 minutes • Cooking time: 45 minutes

2 medium (1 cup) onions, chopped
1 pound ground beef
1 pound pork sausage
1 cup water
1 (28 ounce) can whole tomatoes, undrained, cut up
1 (15 1/2 ounce) can kidney beans, rinsed, drained
1 (15 ounce) can tomato sauce
1 (12 ounce) can tomato paste
2 tablespoons chili powder
1 tablespoon dried basil leaves
1 teaspoon dried oregano leaves
1 teaspoon pepper
1/2 teaspoon salt
3 tablespoons country-style Dijon mustard

8 ounces uncooked dried spaghetti

In 10-inch skillet cook onions, beef and sausage over medium heat until meat is browned (10 to 12 minutes); drain off fat. Meanwhile, in Dutch oven combine all remaining ingredients except spaghetti. Cook over medium heat, stirring occasionally, 15 minutes. Reduce heat to low; add browned meat. Cook, stirring occasionally, until stew is thickened (20 to 30 minutes). Meanwhile, cook spaghetti according to package directions. Rinse with hot water; drain. Serve stew over hot spaghetti. **YIELD:** 6 servings.

Nutrition Information (1 serving): Calories 600; Protein 33g; Carbohydrate 65g; Fat 24g; Cholesterol 75mg; Sodium 2160mg.

Farmhouse Chicken Noodle Stew

A marvelous heart-warming stew.

Preparation time: 15 minutes • Cooking time: 1 hour

1 (3 to 4 pound) frying chicken, cut into 8 pieces
6 cups hot water
1/2 cup chopped fresh parsley
4 stalks (2 cups) celery, sliced 1/4-inch
3 medium carrots, cut into 1-inch pieces
2 medium (1 cup) onions, chopped
2 bay leaves
1 tablespoon dried basil leaves
1 teaspoon dried thyme leaves
1 teaspoon dried marjoram leaves
1 teaspoon salt
1/2 teaspoon pepper
1 (12 ounce) package frozen egg noodles*

In Dutch oven cover chicken with water. Cover; cook over medium high heat for 10 minutes. Add all remaining ingredients except noodles. Cover; cook over medium high heat until chicken is fork tender (20 to 25 minutes). Remove chicken pieces; add noodles. Return to a full boil, skimming off fat during cooking. (Some herbs will be removed.) Meanwhile, remove chicken from bones. Reduce heat to low. Add chicken. Continue cooking until noodles are tender (20 to 25 minutes). Remove bay leaves. **YIELD:** 6 servings.

* 4 ounces (2 cups) uncooked dried egg noodles can be substituted for 1 (12 ounce) package frozen egg noodles.

Nutrition Information (1 serving): Calories 250; Protein 25g; Carbohydrate 23g; Fat 7g; Cholesterol 85mg; Sodium 480mg.

Sauces

Like it spicy?
Try our spaghetti sauce.
Like it creamy?
You'll love our clam sauce.
Like it classy?
Try our wild mushroom
sauce.
And for a little zest,
we've got a pesto version
for you, too.

Spicy Spaghetti Sauce With Pepperoni

A chunky spaghetti sauce that's ready when you are and brimming with flavor.

Preparation time: 10 minutes • Cooking time: 25 minutes *(pictured on page 118)*

1 cup sliced 1/2-inch fresh mushrooms
2 medium (1 cup) onions, chopped
1 cup pitted ripe olives, sliced 1/2-inch
1/2 cup chopped fresh parsley
1 cup water
2 (14 1/2 ounce) cans stewed tomatoes
1 (6 ounce) can tomato paste
2 teaspoons dried basil leaves
1/2 teaspoon dried oregano leaves
1/4 teaspoon pepper
1 tablespoon country-style Dijon mustard
1 teaspoon finely chopped fresh garlic

8 ounces uncooked dried spaghetti

3 ounces sliced pepperoni

In 3-quart saucepan combine all ingredients except spaghetti and pepperoni. Cook over medium heat, stirring occasionally, until sauce is thickened (15 to 20 minutes). Meanwhile, cook spaghetti according to package directions. Rinse with hot water; drain. Stir pepperoni into sauce; continue cooking until heated through (4 to 5 minutes). Serve over hot cooked spaghetti. **YIELD:** 6 servings.

Nutrition Information (1 serving): Calories 300; Protein 10g; Carbohydrate 44g; Fat 10g; Cholesterol 10mg; Sodium 980mg.

Wild Mushroom Sauce

Wild mushrooms are readily available at large or specialty grocery stores.

Preparation time: 15 minutes • Cooking time: 30 minutes

1 cup dry white wine or chicken broth
6 ounces chopped oyster mushrooms or sliced fresh mushrooms
6 ounces chopped shiitake mushrooms or sliced fresh mushrooms
1/4 cup LAND O LAKES® Butter
2 medium (1 cup) onions, chopped
2 medium (2 tablespoons) shallots, finely chopped*
2 tablespoons all-purpose flour
2 cups (1 pint) half-and-half
1 tablespoon chopped mixed fresh herbs (basil, sage, thyme, etc.)**
1/2 teaspoon salt
1/4 teaspoon coarsely ground pepper

Hot cooked pasta

In 10-inch skillet combine wine and mushrooms. Cook over medium high heat, stirring occasionally, until liquid evaporates (10 to 15 minutes). Add butter, onions and shallots; continue cooking, stirring occasionally, until onions are soft (5 to 8 minutes). Stir in flour until smooth and bubbly (1 minute). Stir in half-and-half, fresh herbs, salt and pepper. Continue cooking until sauce is slightly thickened (5 to 6 minutes). Serve over hot cooked pasta. **YIELD:** 3 cups.

* 2 tablespoons chopped onion can be substituted for 2 medium (2 tablespoons) shallots, finely chopped.

** 1 teaspoon mixed dried basil, sage and thyme leaves can be substituted for 1 tablespoon chopped mixed fresh herbs.

Nutrition Information (1/2 cup sauce only): Calories 240; Protein 4g; Carbohydrate 11g; Fat 17g; Cholesterol 50mg; Sodium 290mg.

Creamy White Clam Sauce

Traditionally, this classic Italian sauce is served over fettuccine or linguine.

Preparation time: 10 minutes • Cooking time: 20 minutes

1/3 cup LAND O LAKES® Butter
1 1/2 cups sliced fresh mushrooms
1 medium (1 tablespoon) shallot, finely chopped*
3 tablespoons all-purpose flour
2 (6 1/2 ounce) cans chopped clams, drained, reserve juice
2 cups (1 pint) half-and-half
1/3 cup freshly grated Romano or Parmesan cheese
2 tablespoons chopped fresh chives
1/4 teaspoon coarsely ground pepper
1 tablespoon dry sherry, if desired

Hot cooked pasta

In 3-quart saucepan melt butter until sizzling; add mushrooms and shallot. Cook over medium heat, stirring occasionally, until mushrooms are tender (5 to 7 minutes). Stir in flour until smooth and bubbly (1 minute). Reduce heat to medium low. Gradually add reserved clam juice and half-and-half. Cook, stirring occasionally, until thickened (6 to 10 minutes). Stir in clams, Romano cheese, chives, pepper and sherry. Continue cooking until heated through (1 to 2 minutes). Serve over hot cooked pasta. **YIELD:** 4 cups

* 1 tablespoon chopped onion can be substituted for 1 medium (1 tablespoon) shallot, finely chopped.

Nutrition Information (1/2 cup sauce only): Calories 210; Protein 10g; Carbohydrate 7g; Fat 16g; Cholesterol 65mg; Sodium 200mg.

Fresh Pesto Sauce

Keep this easy and delicious sauce on hand to add flavor to pasta and soup.

Preparation time: 15 minutes

2 cups packed fresh basil leaves
1 (2 ounce) jar (1/3 cup) pine nuts
3 medium cloves fresh garlic
1/3 cup olive or vegetable oil
1/4 cup freshly grated Parmesan cheese
Coarsely ground pepper

Hot cooked pasta

In food processor bowl with metal blade or 5-cup blender container combine basil leaves, pine nuts and garlic. Process until basil is finely chopped (20 to 30 seconds). Slowly add oil through feed tube while food processor is running, until well mixed (20 to 30 seconds). By hand, stir in Parmesan cheese and pepper to taste. Serve pesto tossed with hot cooked pasta. **YIELD:** 3/4 cup.

TIP: Pesto can be stored refrigerated up to 1 week or frozen up to 6 months.

Nutrition Information (1 tablespoon sauce only): Calories 90; Protein 2g; Carbohydrate 2g; Fat 9g; Cholesterol 0mg; Sodium 40mg.

Smoked Bacon Red Sauce Over Spaghetti

Smoked bacon and lots of onions give a delicious, rich flavor to this red sauce.

Preparation time: 10 minutes • Cooking time: 55 minutes

1 pound bacon, cut into 1/2-inch pieces
3 medium (3 cups) onions, thinly sliced
2 teaspoons finely chopped fresh garlic
3/4 cup dry red wine or water
2 (28 ounce) cans Italian or plum tomatoes
1 (12 ounce) can tomato paste
1 tablespoon dried basil leaves
1 teaspoon dried oregano leaves
1 teaspoon coarsely ground pepper
2 bay leaves

8 ounces uncooked dried spaghetti

In Dutch oven cook bacon, onions and garlic over medium high heat, stirring occasionally, until bacon is crisp (8 to 10 minutes); drain off fat. Add all remaining ingredients except spaghetti. Reduce heat to medium; cook, stirring occasionally, until sauce is thickened (40 to 45 minutes). Remove bay leaves. Meanwhile, cook spaghetti according to package directions. Rinse with hot water; drain. Serve red sauce over hot cooked spaghetti. **YIELD:** 6 servings.

Nutrition Information (1 serving): Calories 410; Protein 17g; Carbohydrate 57g; Fat 12g; Cholesterol 18mg; Sodium 1220mg.

Three-Cheese Pasta Sauce

Cream cheese, goat cheese and Parmesan cheese make this sauce three times as good.

Preparation time: 5 minutes • Cooking time: 28 minutes

1/4 cup LAND O LAKES® Butter
2 cups (1 pint) whipping cream
1 (3 ounce) package cream cheese
3 ounces Chevre cheese (soft white goat cheese)*
1/4 teaspoon white pepper
1/8 teaspoon nutmeg
1/4 cup freshly grated Parmesan cheese

Hot cooked pasta
Fresh chopped herbs (rosemary, thyme, basil, etc.)

In 3-quart saucepan melt butter until sizzling; add whipping cream. Cook over medium heat, stirring occasionally, until mixture just comes to a boil (3 to 4 minutes). Reduce heat to low; continue cooking, stirring occasionally, until sauce thickens slightly (15 to 18 minutes). Add cream cheese, Chevre cheese, pepper and nutmeg. Continue cooking, stirring constantly with wire whisk, until cheese is melted (4 to 6 minutes). Stir in Parmesan cheese. Serve over hot cooked pasta; sprinkle with herbs. **YIELD:** 2 cups.

*3 ounces cream cheese plus 1 teaspoon lemon juice can be substituted for 3 ounces Chevre cheese.

Nutrition Information (1/2 cup sauce only): Calories 460; Protein 6g; Carbohydrate 3g; Fat 48g; Cholesterol 165mg; Sodium 270mg,

Index